Do Whatever
He Tells You

Do Whatever He Tells You

Reflections on the Life of Mary

GEORGE B. ANDERSON

BALBOA
PRESS

A DIVISION OF HAY HOUSE

Balboa Press books may be ordered through booksellers or by contacting:

Balboa Press
A Division of Hay House
1663 Liberty Drive
Bloomington, IN 47403
www.balboapress.com
1 (877) 407-4847

Interior Image Credit: Henry Ossawa Tanner; Sandro Botticelli; John Everett Millais; Beverly Paddleford

Print information available on the last page.

ISBN: 978-1-9822-3131-6 (sc)
ISBN: 978-1-9822-3130-9 (hc)
ISBN: 978-1-9822-3137-8 (e)

Library of Congress Control Number: 2019909692

Balboa Press rev. date: 08/02/2019

This book is dedicated
to my beloved wife,
Peggy Anderson
September 29, 1935 – November 7, 2017
"One Faith, One Hope, One Love"

To Begin

Father, we thank you for the gift of
Immaculate Mary, Virgin and God-bearer.
Through your will and the Holy Spirit, she birthed
into the world the gift of Jesus, the Messiah,
your Son and our Savior.

Mary, thank you for your immortal "yes"
and for your life of holiness, faith and courage.
As we learn to love you more deeply, may we also
grow within us some measure of your
courage, faith and holiness.

Contents

Preface

Several factors prompted me to write this book on the life of Mary, the mother of Jesus. Several years ago, I gave a few presentations on this subject. The talks went well, but I came away from the experience realizing that there was so much more to learn about Mary. Indeed, from the Annunciation to the Passion and beyond, her life was extraordinary and has profoundly affected our own lives.

The more I read and studied, the more fascinated I became by the broad impact of Mary's role in salvation history. But as I point out in the introduction, I am not a Scripture scholar or theologian. Far from it! I am simply a Catholic layman with a keen interest in Scripture study. This book is a result of that study and is a series of reflections on the life of Mary. Who is this book written for? It is primarily for my family and close friends, but is also for unknown readers who may come along who share my interest in Mary.

What has intrigued me the most are the periods in Mary's life that are not detailed in Holy Scripture. These are the periods between events such as the Annunciation and Visitation. Following the angel Gabriel's announcement to Mary that she would bear the son of God, she went almost immediately to visit her cousin Elizabeth, a trip on foot of four or five days. Was this travel time a grace to allow her to consider what she had just experienced and what her future might hold? Surely many questions must have flooded her mind, which we will consider in this book. There are many such "open" intervals in her life that make us want to know more. We mustn't invent, but we can consider such periods as we seek to know better the mind and heart of Mary.

I purposely confined myself to the Bible and to commentaries that are similarly based. I avoided the apocryphal (non-canonical) literature. These are works that were written significantly later than the Gospels of Matthew, Mark, Luke and John and are not accepted by the Church as belonging to Holy Scripture. Some of them are interesting and valuable, some are fanciful, but nearly all are outside the purview of this book.

Another interest of mine has been to associate Old Testament writings to the New Testament stories about Mary. For example, readers will notice that at the beginning of most chapters I've placed two Scripture quotations, usually one each from the Old and New Testaments. The Bible from Genesis to Revelation is one complete work; its books are interlinking parts of God's plan for our salvation.

The reader will also find that at the end of each chapter are "Thoughts to Ponder" in the form of questions. They are meant to stimulate thought, prayer and perhaps discussion.

Mary was God's chosen instrument in what we may think of as a joyous mystery uniting heaven and earth in a new way. Her "yes" to the angel Gabriel gave us the incarnate Christ Jesus. This gift was made manifest to us through the faith of a young peasant girl. Mary's life was filled with experiences of joy and happiness, as well as experiences that were difficult and fraught with danger. She lived her life trusting in God and doing his will as well as she could. Throughout her life, she showed that our greatest peace and joy lie in doing the same.

GBA

Introduction

It may seem that the world does not need another book about Mary, the mother of Jesus. For nearly two thousand years, more than any other woman in history, Mary has been honored with paintings, music, sculptures, shrines and churches. She has been memorialized in many books, films and other media. Why yet another book?

This writing started as a personal exercise. As my spiritual life matured, I wanted to know more about this person who lived such an extraordinarily grace-filled life, but a life that was filled also with challenge, mystery and danger. Mary's experiences were clearly beyond any experiences of mine. Visited by God's messenger, the angel Gabriel, only once that we know of from Scripture, she lived her life toward an uncertain future with faith, hope, love and courage.

Why is Mary so important to us? With her *fiat*, her "yes," she conceived through the Holy Spirit and welcomed Jesus into her womb. With her own flesh and blood, she gave life to the incarnate Christ. Her DNA was a part of him. At the Council of Ephesus, held in 431 A.D., the Church proclaimed Mary as *Theotokos*, the Mother of God. As Jon Sweeney put it in his book *Strange Heaven*, "Mary is the mother of one, united person, who is Jesus Christ, both God and man."[1]

Mary was with Jesus throughout his earthly life. She nurtured and raised him, taught and protected him. She was his first disciple and later called him into his public ministry. Mary bore witness to his crucifixion. Still later, she rejoiced with his disciples at his resurrection and at all it would mean for the world.

Another reason Mary is so important is that she is foreshadowed in the Old Testament. The mythic Eve of Genesis can be said to prefigure Mary, who is sometimes called "the new Eve." Created without sin, Eve chose to disobey God and, with Adam, succumbed to the temptation to become godlike herself. Sin thus entered a previously unblemished world. Mary, also born without sin, made a very different choice. She chose to obey God's will, thereby opening a path to redemption from sin.

We may think of the Old and New Testaments as being distinct from each other—the "old" from the "new." But as St. Augustine (354-430) wrote, "The New Testament is concealed in the Old, and the Old is revealed in the New."[2] If we ignore the Old Testament, we miss critical insights into our spiritual heritage. We should acknowledge that our Jewish brothers and sisters see the Old Testament, the Hebrew Bible, as speaking specifically to them as the Chosen People, bound by a covenant with God. We Christians see the Old Testament as also foreshadowing a new covenant with God as his adopted sons and daughters. Both covenants are true, and God does not break his covenants.

One of the Old Testament passages most frequently quoted by Christians is a prophecy by Isaiah. Read literally, it concerns King Ahaz of Judah, of the house of David. The narrative dates to about 735 B.C. and describe Ahaz's dilemma when Judah is threatened by two northern kingdoms. Isaiah tells Ahaz to ask for a sign that God is with him. Ahaz insists that he will not test the Lord by asking for one, to which the prophet impatiently responds, *"Therefore the Lord himself will give you a sign: The virgin will be with child and will give birth to a son, and will call him Immanuel"* (Isaiah 7:14). In the New Testament, the Gospel writer Matthew applies this prophecy to Jesus: *"All this took place to fulfill what the Lord had said through the prophet: 'The virgin will be with child and will give birth to a son, and they will call him Immanuel'—which means, 'God with us'"* (Matthew 1:22-23). Scholars and theologians may debate the interpretation, but for many Christians, the Isaiah prophecy adopted by Matthew predicts the coming of Jesus.

There are other parallels that may be drawn between the Old and New Testaments. For example, in Exodus there is a detailed description of the Ark of the Covenant (Exodus 25:10-22). Within the Ark were two stone tablets containing the Ten Commandments given by God to Moses. The Ark thus contained the Word of God and the guiding law for the Israelites. It was their holy treasure. Mary, the Immaculate Conception, born without sin, is sometimes referred to as the Ark of the New Covenant, since she held within her womb Jesus, the Word made flesh. Thus, Mary holds a pivotal role in the salvation of humanity!

Salvation history is a linear narrative, written by many different authors over a thousand years—about 900 years in the Old Testament and about 100 years in the New Testament. Through many generations from Abraham to today, people have slowly come to a deeper understanding of the inspired words of God in Sacred Scripture. Truth stands on its own. It is absolute. However, some truths are only fully comprehended after a long time. For example, in the American colonies' Declaration of Independence we read, "We hold these truths to be self-evident: that all men are created equal, that they are endowed by their Creator with certain unalienable Rights, that among these are Life, Liberty and the pursuit of Happiness." It was a bold and thrilling claim when first declared in 1776. But what it was understood to mean at the time was that all white men with property were created equal! Equality did not extend to women, Native Americans, or other people of color. But over time, society came to question and then to challenge the conventional understanding of the original declaration. Thus, there came about the abolition of slavery, women's suffrage, civil rights laws and a deeper understanding of what "All men are created equal" really means.

So it has been with the truths revealed in the Bible. It is all there: God's revealed truth and plan for our salvation. But human beings have proven to be slow learners. Surely we can all now agree that slavery is wrong even though it was once considered acceptable and even justified by certain Scripture passages. Truth needs to be studied, questioned and pondered to be fully understood. Even so, we can read and reread treasured passages of the Bible and yet not fully comprehend the truth embedded therein. It is like looking into a treasure chest but not seeing or comprehending all the treasure it holds.

For another example, we read in the Old Testament: *"But if there is serious injury, you are to take life for life, eye for eye, tooth for tooth"* (Exodus 21:23-24). This was perhaps an attempt, however harsh, to limit retaliation to the specific crime. Jesus recalled this passage when he instructed his followers, *"You have heard that it was said, 'Eye for eye, and tooth for tooth.' But I tell you, Do not resist an evil person. If someone strikes you on the right cheek, turn to him the other also"* (Matthew 5:38-39). In so doing he revealed a deeper understanding of the truth bound into justice.

The concept of the Holy Trinity is another example of a truth revealed in the Bible and understood more completely over time. The word Trinity does not occur in the Bible, but Matthew quotes Jesus as saying, *"Go and make disciples of all nations, baptizing them in the name of the Father and of the Son and of the Holy Spirit"* (Matthew 28:18-19). And the Apostle Paul writes, *"May the grace of the Lord Jesus Christ, and the love of God, and the fellowship of the Holy Spirit be with you all"* (2 Corinthians 13:14). However, it wasn't until the Council of Nicaea in 325 A.D. that the doctrine of the mystery of the Holy Trinity was formally promulgated via the Nicene Creed.

Think for a moment of Zechariah and Elizabeth. Zechariah was told the truth by an angel that his aged and childless wife, Elizabeth, would bear a son. Can we blame him for not understanding or immediately believing? All he had was his life's experience to draw upon; for Elizabeth to give birth at her age was seemingly impossible. The angel told him the truth, but it took time for Zechariah to understand and believe the truth of that message. Certainly, when Elizabeth did indeed become pregnant that was proof enough!

Mary was also told the truth by an angel. She may not have fully comprehended what Gabriel told her, but she put her trust in God and accepted his invitation. Like Eve, this young woman was faced with a choice. She could say "no" and retreat to the security of her family and the fulfillment of her marriage to Joseph. Or she could say "yes" and accept all the challenges, unknowns and potential dangers that this would entail. *"'I am the Lord's servant,' Mary answered. 'May it be to me as you have said'"* (Luke 1:38). The Bible in its entirety from

Genesis to Revelation is God's revealed plan of salvation. Mary thus became the keystone in the arch between the Old Testament time of foreshadowing and the New Testament time of fulfillment. Had Mary said "no," the connection would have been broken. Salvation history would have been broken! She is the link that made the coming of Jesus possible. Mary's "yes" was made through the exercise of her own free will, graced by her own faith and trust in God.

Just as Mary thoughtfully pondered what had been revealed to her, so should we! I hope that in the chapters which follow the reader will do just that and, in the process, discover a deeper faith and a greater awareness of God's love.

This book explores Mary's earthly life as she lived, worked and walked among the people. There is little information in Scripture to illuminate her life, but much to ponder. In fact, Mary's last words recorded in Scripture were at the wedding at Cana: *"Do whatever he tells you"* (John 2:5). The Gospels of Matthew and Luke are the most revealing of Mary's life. Mark mentions her by name only once (Mark 6:3) and another time refers to her as "Jesus' mother" (Mark 3:31). John also refers to her simply as "Jesus' mother" (John 2:1).

The Gospels were written by different authors at different times for different audiences. Accordingly, in this reflection on the life of Mary I have tried to avoid comingling their accounts. This may cause some unease for readers who are used to a more integrated narrative. Yet we need to recognize that there are significant differences between the Gospel accounts. For example, Luke describes the visit of the shepherds but makes no mention of Magi. Matthew describes the Magi with no reference to shepherds. There are other differences which will be discussed in the appropriate chapters (see also Appendix A for a comparison of Matthew and Luke). To put a finer point on this issue, I quote from the late Biblical scholar, Fr. Raymond E. Brown, S.S.:

> As we look back on the Lucan infancy narrative, inevitably there is a tendency to compare it to the Matthean. Throughout I have insisted that the two

stories are very different, that neither evangelist knew the other's work, and that efforts at harmonizing the narratives into one consecutive story are quite impossible. But beneath the differences and even irreconcilability, there is a common understanding of the birth of the Messiah.[3]

Both Gospel accounts are critical to knowing Mary better and to helping us consider what might have transpired between the events described in Scripture. There are no definitive answers to the questions this book asks about those times. But by considering them, we can reach a deeper appreciation of who Mary is and what she means to us. However, a caution is in order. I have found it helpful to ponder the undocumented periods in Mary's life, but only within the context of the details provided by Scripture.

We are, in our modern, first world culture, a visual people. Books can inform but movies illuminate ideas. In my view, the 2012 film, *Mary of Nazareth*, directed by Giacomo Campiotti and starring Alissa Jung, is the most compelling film portrayal of Mary yet produced.[4] The director took some liberties by using imagery of the child Mary drawn from the apocryphal Gospel of James. It is not necessarily wrong to do so. But a reader, or in this case a viewer, needs to know this has been done to fill in some of the gaps in Mary's story.

Without apology let me state that this is a simple book. It is not a theological treatise. It is written simply to consider Mary as she really lived while giving us the gift of her son, Jesus. Each chapter focuses on an important event in Mary's life. These events (and the intervals between events) invite us to reflect and pray. If that happens, this book will have served its purpose.

Scriptural quotations are taken from the New International Version (NIV) Study Bible, unless otherwise noted.[5]

Chapter One

Zechariah, Elizabeth and John

A voice of one calling: "In the desert prepare the way for the Lord;
make straight in the wilderness a highway for our God."

Isaiah 40:3

"Your wife Elizabeth will bear you a son, and you are to give him the
name John. He will be a joy and delight to you, and many will rejoice
because of his birth, for he will be great in the sight of the Lord."

Luke 1:13-15

From the Gospel of Luke

Luke begins his Gospel with the story of Zechariah, Elizabeth and their promised son, John. It precedes the Annunciation to Mary by about six months. It is compelling to consider how the events surrounding this elderly couple are linked to the later birth of Jesus and to his mission. Individual events may not at first be seen as parts of the whole. But once they are linked together a picture emerges of what we are meant to see and to understand from Sacred Scripture.

Zechariah (whose name means "Yahweh remembers") was a priest from the ancestral line of Aaron, in the tribe of Levi. The tribe of Levi was designated to provide priestly service to the other eleven tribes of Israel. It had twenty-four divisions dispersed throughout the land wherever the tribes had settled. Each division was quite large, comprised of upward of a thousand priests. Zechariah belonged to the division of Abijah and had been chosen by lot to attend to the morning and evening rituals in the Temple by praying and burning incense for a week. It may have been the only time this sacred duty fell to him. He would be in the Temple alone, praying and honoring God on behalf of his people.

While Zechariah was thus engaged, the angel Gabriel suddenly appeared and said to him, *"Do not be afraid, Zechariah; your prayer has been heard"* (Luke 1:13). We are told that he was indeed *"gripped with fear"* (Luke 1:12). Then he was told the most astounding news:

> *"Your wife Elizabeth will bear you a son, and you are to give him the name John. He will be a joy and delight to you, and many will rejoice because of his birth, for he will be great in the sight of the Lord. He is never to take wine or other fermented drink, and he will be filled with the Holy Spirit even from birth."*
>
> Luke 1:13-15

It was news that must have been difficult to comprehend. He and his wife were already old. They had been childless throughout their marriage, and Elizabeth was now well past childbearing age. Zechariah was a faithful priest. But try to put yourself in his place. Wouldn't you be startled and question the angel just as he did? *"How can I be sure of this? I am an old man and my wife is well along in years"* (Luke 1:18). Notice Zechariah's challenge to Gabriel: "How can I be *sure* of this?" He wants confirming information, which the angel does not provide. Instead, Gabriel tells him he will be unable to speak until the child is born, as punishment for his disbelief.

I wonder if Zechariah's punishment might have been a blessing in disguise for his community. When he left the Temple, he was unable to offer the expected priestly blessing to the assembled worshipers. It became apparent to them that something extraordinary, something profoundly spiritual, had happened. They realized that he had seen a vision. Perhaps in the hearts and minds of the local community, temple worship was validated and the role of the priests was affirmed. But everyone had to wait to learn what this strange occurrence might mean.

When his week of service in the Temple had ended, Zechariah returned home, and Elizabeth became pregnant. She remained in seclusion for five months. This must have given her time to realize that she and her husband were participating in a unique plan of God. She had been childless her whole life. For a Jewish woman in those times, this was considered disgraceful. It was often assumed that if a woman was childless it was because God was displeased with her. In fact, if a wife did not bear children, her husband had legal grounds to divorce her. Childlessness was always assumed to be the "fault" of the wife, never of the husband! It had surely caused talk among the other villagers. "Why has God not blessed Elizabeth with children?" they might have gossiped. "And she the wife of a priest," others might have added. Then in old age she suddenly became pregnant! Luke records her reflection on this miracle: *The Lord has done this for me … In these days he has shown his favor and taken away my disgrace among the people*" (Luke 1:25).

Others before Elizabeth had had miraculous pregnancies late in life. Think of Abraham's wife Sarah. She overheard the Lord telling her husband that she would have a son, at which she laughed and thought, *"After I am worn out and my master is old, will I now have this pleasure?"* (Genesis 18:12). The Lord heard her laugh and responded, *"Is anything too hard for the Lord?"* (Genesis 18:14), at which she grew thoughtful and fearful. The prophecy soon came true when her son Isaac was born (Genesis 21:1-3).

Hannah, the wife of Elkanah, after many years of childlessness had fervently prayed,

> *"O Lord Almighty, if you will only look upon your servant's misery and remember me, and not forget your servant but give her a son, then I will give him to the Lord for all the days of his life, and no razor will ever be used on his head."*
>
> 1 Samuel 1:11

Blessed with a son, Samuel, she honored her vow. After weaning her son, she dedicated him to the Lord in the Temple, where he was raised. Samuel would later serve God as a prophet. The story of John the Baptist in many ways parallels that of Samuel.

Now Zechariah and Elizabeth, also late in life, were to have a son. Three elderly women—Sarah and Hannah in the Old Testament and Elizabeth in the New Testament—were each favored by God with a son, each for a special purpose.

Perhaps Elizabeth wondered if at her age she would be able to carry the baby to full term and to a healthy birth. Although he could not speak, Zechariah surely indicated to her through signs what he had experienced in the Temple. He must have shared that the baby was to be called John and was destined for greatness in God's eyes. She would come to understand that because God had decreed John's future, she would indeed carry him to a healthy birth. Zechariah's inability to speak and Elizabeth's seclusion gave them both the opportunity to ponder God's manifest presence. A lesson observed might be that we all need quiet time to discern God's presence in our lives.

Why were Zechariah and Elizabeth chosen to bear the son who would prepare a way for Jesus? Luke relates that they were both descendants of Aaron, the brother of Moses and first High Priest of the Israelites. They were diligent in observing the Law of Moses. Their fidelity to God and to each other was well established. As Fr. Brown notes,

> Combining priestly origins and blameless observance
> of the Law, Zechariah and Elizabeth were for Luke
> the representatives of the best in the religion of Israel;
> and as a remnant which received the "good news" ...
> they personified the continuity in salvation history.[6]

This is in reference to Israelis who returned to Judah to rebuild Jerusalem after the Babylonian Captivity. Zechariah and Elizabeth were descendents of this "remnant" of the Jewish people.

Following the story of the angel's appearance to Zechariah and Elizabeth's pregnancy, Luke relates the story of how Gabriel appeared to Mary and her own miraculous pregnancy just six months later, creating parallels and resonance between the two events. Luke then recounts Mary's visit to Elizabeth, while both women were pregnant, before proceeding to the birth of John. I have chosen to treat the Annunciation and Visitation in subsequent chapters, but it is important to note that Luke weaves these episodes together with the story of Elizabeth's pregnancy and the birth of John.

The news of Elizabeth's pregnancy and the birth of her son would have been a shock to the villagers. As Luke says, *"Her neighbors and relations heard that the Lord had shown her great mercy, and they shared her joy"* (Luke 1:58).

Perhaps they connected her pregnancy with Zechariah's inability to speak following his service in the Temple. Eight days after his birth, when they came for the boy's circumcision, they tried to name him after his father. But Elizabeth declared that he would be named John. As biblical scholar William Barclay notes, "John is a shorter form of the name *Jehohanan*, which means *Jehovah's gift* or *God is gracious*."[7] Zechariah quickly confirmed what his wife had said by writing on a slate, *"His name is John"* (Luke 1:63). Suddenly his power of speech returned, to everyone's amazement.

Years after "meeting" his cousin when they were both in the womb, John would baptize Jesus in the River Jordan. Did the cousins meet at other times? We do not know. We do know that John dedicated his life in service to God. As a visible sign of his dedication he lived as a Nazirite, just as Samuel did; that is, he never drank alcohol or cut his hair (Judges 13:5). As he pursued his ministry, John's reputation would grow. He would become the last of the great prophets (i.e., those who are entrusted with the inspired word of God).

Slowly, the picture Luke paints begins to take shape. Elizabeth will be a confirming sign to Mary that all things are indeed possible with God. And in time, John will become a voice in the land calling for a new repentance: *"Prepare the way for the Lord, make straight paths for him"* (Luke 3:4). John the Baptist echoes the prophecy of Isaiah to point the way to Jesus the Messiah (Isaiah 40:3).

Following Mary's visit, Zechariah and Elizabeth do not appear again in the New Testament. But Zechariah left us with a prophetic and moving prayer, described in Appendix B. The Canticle of Zechariah remains an important daily prayer for the Church.

Next, we will turn toward the village of Nazareth and to a remarkable visit by God's timeless messenger, Gabriel, to a young Jewish peasant girl.

Thoughts to Ponder

- Jewish women were expected to marry and to provide their husbands with children, particularly sons. The psychological burden on a woman who was childless was very painful. Sarah, Hannah and Elizabeth knew this pain and may even have felt abandoned by God, but they remained faithful to him. Today, in our fast-moving world with its demands for instant gratification, could we endure the years of longing and waiting while remaining faithful and trusting? How patient with God are you?

- Nazirites like John showed their dedication to God by not cutting their hair and abstaining from alcohol (Numbers 6:1-8). Those living as Nazirites were thus identifiable and respected. Today, most clergy wear clothing or symbols appropriate to their calling as outward signs of their vocation. Lay people from all walks of life often wear symbols of their faith. What, if anything, do you consider an appropriate outward sign of your faith?

- After years of longing, Elizabeth and Zechariah were finally blessed with a son. Normally a son would take care of his parents in their final years. Yet they gave John, their "firstborn son," to God. Parents today may be asked to give their blessing if their child senses a call to live a consecrated life as a sister, brother or priest. For some families this may cause conflicted feelings. Parents look forward to having grandchildren, yet the religious life can also bring great joy to parents of a son or daughter who is called to serve the Lord and his people. How do you feel about this in your own family?

Chapter Two

The Annunciation

*"Therefore the Lord himself will give you a sign: the virgin will be
with child and will give birth to a son, and will call him Immanuel."*

Isaiah 7:14

*"Do not be afraid, Mary, you have found favor with
God. You will be with child and give birth to a son,
and you are to give him the name Jesus."*

Luke 1:30-31

From the Gospel of Luke

Consider Mary in the context of her religious and cultural background.
She grew up in the village of Nazareth in the southern part of Galilee,
about sixteen miles west of the Sea of Galilee. Scholars estimate
its population at that time to be between two hundred and four
hundred inhabitants.[8] The fabric of this community was tightly

woven. Everyone knew everyone. Family news became everyone's news. Families were interconnected through marriage. All were of the same observant Jewish faith. Gathering times were story telling times. Travel from the village was limited to an annual journey to Jerusalem for Passover, to local markets and to the nearby town of Sepphoris. Sepphoris was growing in importance as a commercial center with marketplaces to buy and sell produce and other goods.

The people of Nazareth were hardworking. Farming was the main occupation. Wheat, flax, olives and dates were important crops. What would Mary's upbringing in such a community be like? As scholar Jean-Pierre Isbouts writes,

> Mary's mother would have prepared her daughter for the manifold duties of a wife early on. From age six or seven onward, Mary would have helped her mother with simple duties involving cooking, kneading dough for bread, washing, feeding the animals, and taking care of the younger children. At harvest time, she was expected to help her parents pick the fruits from their orchard and learn to carefully crush the olives for the production of olive oil. On market day, Mary would have accompanied her mother to the nearest market to help sell their surplus yields.[9]

Marriage traditionally was arranged by the parents. Girls were considered to be physically mature and of marriageable age at around fourteen or fifteen years. Apparently, Mary's parents, Anne and Joachim,* approved of Joseph. Luke tells us that Mary, a virgin, was pledged to be married to Joseph, a descendant of David (Luke 1:27). The whole village knew of the betrothal. The wedding was being planned. But as we know, there was a surprise coming: a holy surprise!

---

* Mary's parents' names come from the apocryphal (non-canonical) Gospel of James, also called the Protoevangelium. According to tradition they were both from the tribe of Judah and descendants of the House of David.

The Annunciation story appears in the Gospel of Luke. It has also been portrayed for generations of Christians in paintings, frescoes, mosaics, stained glass and sculpture. Many of these depictions are precious to us and are correctly called sacred art. Paintings of the Annunciation by Giotto, Fra Angelico, Botticelli and Raphael are considered to be among the world's finest works of art.

Such paintings usually depict Mary as a European noblewoman with fair skin and blond or light brown hair and dressed in elegant robes. They remind me of an experience I had as a young naval officer when I visited a tiny Catholic church north of the Arctic Circle in the fishing village of Tromsø, Norway. Next to the altar was a painting of the Blessed Virgin. She was portrayed as a tall, strong-boned woman, with a fair complexion and golden hair in traditional Norwegian braids. Historically accurate? I think not. She looked every bit the young Viking princess. Depictions of Mary tend to reflect each artist's own time and place. A fascinating time can be spent online discovering the many beautiful images of Mary created by artists from every culture where Mary is honored.

Much less frequently do we see Mary depicted as she truly was: a young Middle Eastern woman. One beautiful example of this is by the African American artist Henry Ossawa Tanner, who painted *The Annunciation* in 1898. In a welcome and interesting exception to the norm, Tanner's painting shows Mary as we might imagine her living in her country village.

In this painting, perhaps the first thing one notices is the shaft of blazing light that represents God's messenger, the angel Gabriel. Powerful as the light is, our attention is drawn to the youthful Mary. Her eyes are fixed on Gabriel, her hands gently clasped, and she is sitting as though just awakened. As Luke recounts, Mary is *"greatly troubled"* by the angel's greeting (Luke 1:29). He continues,

> *"Do not be afraid, Mary, you have found favor with God. You will be with child and give birth to a son, and you are to give him the name Jesus. He will be great and will be called the Son of the Most High. The Lord*

God will give him the throne of his father David, and
he will reign over the house of Jacob forever; his kingdom
will never end."

Luke 1:30-33

The Annunciation, by H. O. Tanner.
Courtesy Philadelphia Museum of Art, purchased
by the W.P. Wilstach Fund, W1899-1-1

In this painting Mary does not seem fearful. Rather, there is a quiet pondering, or as Tanner's biographer Marcia Mathews writes, "She sits on her bed with hands clasped and looks with an expression of receptive wonder toward the miraculous vision which is conveyed by a shaft of golden light."[10] Marcus Bruce in his biography of Tanner writes, "It is Mary's openness and willing response to the news, a receptivity revealed in her body language, that is most revealing and profound about this painting."[11] She appears to be thinking about what she has just been told. Perplexed, she asks a simple but logical question, *"How will this be ... since I am a virgin?"* (Luke 1:34). Notice that she asks how *will* this be, not how *can* this be. She is already in the affirmative. Gabriel replies, *"The Holy Spirit will come upon you, and the power of the Most High will overshadow you. So the holy one to be born will be called the Son of God"* (Luke 1:35). Gabriel waits for her reply. *"'I am the Lord's servant,' Mary answered. 'May it be to me as you have said'"* (Luke 1:38).

Let us leave Scripture for a moment. We need to reflect on the meaning of the Annunciation and Mary's *fiat* for humankind and for all time. This is a heart stopping, profound moment in salvation history. Metaphorically, all humanity, along with the angels, collectively held their breath awaiting Mary's reply. The salvation of humanity was hanging in the balance and depended upon her answer. Mary, chosen by the Father before she was born and given the fullness of grace, nevertheless had the power and free will to say no to God. Otherwise she would not have been asked. Nor would her "yes" have had any meaning!

St. Bernard of Clairvaux (1090-1153) expressed the power of the moment beautifully:

> You have heard, O Virgin, that you will conceive and
>   bear a son;
> you have heard that it will not be by man but by the
>   Holy Spirit.
> The angel awaits an answer; it is time for him to
>   return to God who sent him.
> We too are waiting, O Lady, for your word of
>   compassion;
>
> the sentence of condemnation weighs heavily upon us.
> The price of our salvation is offered to you.
> We shall be set free at once if you consent.
> In the eternal Word of God, we all came to be, and
>   behold, we die.

In your brief response we are to be remade in order to be recalled to life.

Tearful Adam with his sorrowing family begs this of you, O loving Virgin,
in their exile from Paradise. Abraham begs it, David begs it.
All the other holy patriarchs, your ancestors, ask it of you,
as they dwell in the country of the shadow of death.
This is what the whole earth waits for, prostrate at your feet.
It is right in doing so, for on your word depends comfort for the wretched,
ransom for the captive, freedom for the condemned, indeed,
salvation for all the sons of Adam, the whole of your race.

Answer quickly, O Virgin.
Reply in haste to the angel, or rather through the angel to the Lord.
Answer with a word, receive the Word of God.
Speak your own word, conceive the divine Word.
Breathe a passing word, embrace the eternal Word.[12]

Again, we recall Mary's response: *"I am the Lord's servant ... May it be to me as you have said"* (Luke 1:38). It is a thoughtful and faith-filled answer, the answer of someone who knows her own mind. Her only desire was to be obedient to God's will. Along with her family and neighbors, indeed all of Israel, Mary eagerly anticipated the coming of the Messiah. Her upbringing and spiritual development as a devout Jewish woman would have been thorough. Although she was young, Mary was a person of remarkable inner strength and will. She did not first go to her parents, to whom she was subject, to ask them what she should do. She pondered Gabriel's message and made up her own mind. Then she committed to God's invitation to bear the Son of God. We can imagine all humanity and the angels letting out a collective sigh of relief!

Perhaps for a moment we might reflect on God's will and our free will. God, being omniscient, knew Mary before she was even born. From the moment of her conception onward, she was graced by God. Clearly God chose her to receive his invitation through Gabriel. This was God's will. The grace that Mary possessed was to be unconditionally open to God's will. Most of us hope or try to do God's will, but usually we hold back a little. Mary never held back. Did she have the ability (the free will) to refuse the invitation? Yes! There is always a tension between God's will for us and our freedom to refuse it. Mary chose to say "yes": *"May it be to me as you have said."*

Mary's *fiat* became a bridge between the Old and New Testaments. With her "yes," God's plan of redemptive salvation could now move forward. A new holy covenant between God and humanity through Christ Jesus could be established. The foreshadowing and prophecies written in the Old Testament could be brought to life, as recorded in the New Testament.

What thoughts must have gone through Mary's mind following Gabriel's departure? She had been visited by God's messenger; of this she had no doubt. It was a message and an invitation from God to her alone! Before she could even begin to think of the problems she might face, she must have experienced incredible wonder and sublime joy. God had invited her to give birth to the long-awaited Messiah. She heard the words but surely it would take some time to comprehend their full meaning. God's love and her love were joined in a moment of absolute truth beyond human understanding. Soon enough she would encounter problems concerning her unexpected pregnancy. But for now, this precious, private moment of being one with God was hers. God knew her and had chosen her to give birth to the Messiah! It must have been a moment of intense, intimate joy.

Despite the joy of knowing she had been selected by God, the challenges that lay ahead must have been daunting. In her culture and at her age, betrothed but not yet living with Joseph, what could she do? To whom could she tell her extraordinary news? Presumably she would have confided in her mother. Did Anne in turn tell her husband Joachim? If so, what was his reaction? According to Jewish law and custom, the husband had authority over his wife and children. Did Anne and Joachim believe their daughter was pregnant by Joseph or by the Holy Spirit? When did they come to accept that their daughter was carrying the longed-for Messiah?

And when did Mary tell Joseph? Was it before Mary left to visit Elizabeth and Zechariah or when she returned home? Whenever Joseph was told, it must have been the most unbelievable and heart-rending news. How could he believe her? Tradition suggests Joseph was a kind man who loved Mary. Perhaps he encouraged her to leave town and go visit Elizabeth, both for her safety and so he could figure out what to do next. Or perhaps he knew nothing about her condition until she returned to Nazareth.

Mary, though still very young, had a quiet strength and the courage to accomplish this new mission in her life. The journey to Elizabeth and Zechariah would take several days, time for Mary to begin to process what was happening to her. How did she come to understand the enormity of what was happening and why she should be so honored? Surely these thoughts and many more were with her as she traveled south to Judea.

Thoughts to Ponder

- We are all called to become holy. We may aspire to holiness, but it is more often an ideal than a reality. With Mary the ideal and reality were one and the same. More than anything else, it helps to explain her courage and her ability to answer "yes" to God. To say "yes" to God in faith and trust is our challenge, too. Sometimes we hesitate or even turn away from where God is calling us. Have you experienced God calling you? How did you respond?

- Mary experienced moments of intense joy, not simply happiness. Such moments can be ours, too. The secret is love given and received at the same time. Lovers know this. A mother with a baby in her arms knows this. A father seeing his newborn child for the first time knows this. Such moments of joy may steal into our lives if we are open to love without reservation. What moments of joy do you remember and treasure?

- Mary was asked to accept in faith something that at first may have seemed impossible. Yet she responded with how *"will"* this be done, not how *"can"* this be done. Her faith in God was evident in her response: *"May it be to me as you have said."* That is the very definition of a trusting faith in God. Like Mary, we are asked to accept in faith things that reason tells us should not be possible. How do you reconcile the demands of reason and faith?

- We've heard the stories of the Annunciation and Nativity since childhood, perhaps without thinking much about the angels. Years ago my elderly uncle, Fr. Ron Anderson, lay dying. A parishioner was sitting by his bedside. Fr. Ron was stirring and the friend asked him what was happening. "They're coming," he said. "Who is coming?" the friend asked. "The angels," he replied, and fell back asleep. A little later he was stirring again. His friend again asked him what was happening. Fr. Ron muttered, "They're here," and died! Do you believe in angels?

Chapter Three

The Visitation

My soul will boast in the Lord; let the afflicted hear and rejoice.
Glorify the Lord with me; let us exalt his name together.

Psalms 34:2-3

"Even Elizabeth your relative is going to have a child in
her old age, and she who was said to be barren is in her
sixth month. For nothing is impossible with God."

Luke 1:36-37

From the Gospel of Luke

We continue with the Gospel of Luke because it provides the only
account of Mary's visit to her cousin Elizabeth. It tells of a critically
important time in Mary's life and in the lives of Zechariah's family.
It offers much to reflect upon as this young woman began to consider

what she had agreed to do. She had agreed to bear a child who would be known as the Son of the Most High!

We might first consider why Mary, so soon after the Annunciation, went to visit her cousin Elizabeth. Gabriel had told her, *"Even Elizabeth your relative is going to have a child in her old age, and she who was said to be barren is in her sixth month. For nothing is impossible with God"* (Luke 1:36-37). Mary surely wanted to see for herself the miracle that Gabriel had described, and to be with the one person who more than any other could understand what she herself was experiencing.

There may have been additional reasons for the visit, such as Mary's concern for Elizabeth, knowing that she would need help. Maybe Mary needed time away to consider the incredible responsibility she now had. Maybe she had told her parents of Gabriel's visit and they thought it best for her to leave for a while. Perhaps she went to be protected from gossiping tongues in her village, knowing that her pregnancy would soon become public knowledge.

In any case, what a gift that Mary could turn to her cousin at this time! Elizabeth would be a living sign to all that God can accomplish anything. Mary would have someone to confide in and to help, and Elizabeth with the wisdom of her years could in turn help Mary.

In any event, shortly after the Annunciation, she did go to visit Elizabeth: *"Mary got ready and hurried to a town in the hill country of Judea"* (Luke 1:39). Presumably she traveled on foot from Nazareth, or perhaps on a donkey, although it seems unlikely that she would take a working animal away from home for an extended period. Biblical scholars point to the village of Ein Karem, near Jerusalem, as her probable destination. Even today Ein Karem is visited by pilgrims as the hometown of Zechariah and Elizabeth.

From Nazareth in the district of Galilee to Ein Karem south of Samaria and into Judea is about eighty miles, depending on Mary's route around Samaria. The trip is a time in Mary's life that is hidden from us. We can only imagine what she was thinking during her journey south from Nazareth. It would take at least four or five days to get there. Groups frequently traveled south from Galilee to Jerusalem. Traveling with a group would offer some measure of safety, which would have been important for a young woman. Perhaps Mary knew some of her fellow travelers. But this would not have been a time for much conversation, so soon after the Annunciation. Nor would it be a time to confide in others. I imagine that Mary would have been deeply introspective and solitary in her thoughts.

Her thoughts would have been on what Gabriel had said to her and on what lay ahead. He had told her nothing about what to do next. Her marriage to Joseph was already planned and announced. Under Jewish custom they were considered married during the betrothal period but did not yet live together. Would he believe she had become pregnant by the Holy Spirit? Would he stand by her, or would she and her child be alone to face the world? Would her cousin Elizabeth believe her? Would Zechariah accept her into his home once he learned she was pregnant? How would she find the words to tell them about the angel's invitation? The moments of joy she had experienced at being one with God must have been sublime, but now the reality of her new life and its challenges may have felt daunting. And yet the grace of being chosen by God must also have kept flooding back to her. This was a precious and important private time for Mary, a time of wonderment, prayer and questioning. We are left to wonder about this very special, introspective time Mary had on her way to Ein Karem. "Dear God," she might have prayed, "Help me to understand this journey."

Elizabeth had remained in seclusion for the first five months of her pregnancy. Mary arrived during Elizabeth's sixth month. Luke vividly describes their meeting:

> *When Elizabeth heard Mary's greeting, the baby leaped in her womb, and Elizabeth was filled with the Holy Spirit. In a loud voice she exclaimed: "Blessed are you among women, and blessed is the child you will bear! But why am I so favored, that the mother of my Lord should come to me? As soon as the sound of your greeting reached my ears, the baby in my womb leaped for joy. Blessed is she who has believed that what the Lord has said to her will be accomplished!"*
> Luke 1:41-45

"Elizabeth was filled with the Holy Spirit"—inspired by the Holy Spirit might be another way to explain her awareness of Mary's condition. It was as if she had been present herself to hear the angel's message to Mary. When Elizabeth's baby leaped in her womb, she realized with profound joy that Mary was the mother of her Lord, the long-awaited Messiah!

Elizabeth's concluding words to her were, *"Blessed is she who has believed that what the Lord has said to her will be accomplished."* Mary herself acknowledged this by replying, *"From now on all generations will call me blessed"* (Luke 1:48), meaning that she was blessed not because of herself, but because she would give birth to Jesus. She would be responsible for nurturing him through childhood and into adulthood. Both Mary and Elizabeth were profoundly aware of what God had revealed to them. Elizabeth became the first person in Scripture to declare Mary *"the mother of my Lord."*

Luke then relates how Mary responded to Elizabeth with an elegant prayer glorifying God. Known as the Magnificat (after the first word in the Latin version of the poem), it is one of three "canticles" or songs in Luke's Gospel. Indeed, canticles are called by some "Lucan hymns." Luke's Gospel comes to us from his inspired writing. Luke, in memorializing the story of Mary, tried to convey what he heard she had said and what came to him from various sources, perhaps even from Mary herself, in a manner consistent with the heightened emotion of the scene.

Most people in Mary's time were taught the Scriptures through oral tradition. The Torah, the Prophets and the Psalms were taught, prayed, sung and selectively memorized. These writings meant everything to the Jewish people; they were the very essence of their beliefs and culture. A Jewish woman, praying to conceive or to give thanks for childbirth, may have taken to heart Hannah's prayer from the Book of Samuel and memorized it. It begins:

> *"My heart rejoices in the Lord;*
> *in the Lord my horn is lifted high.*
> *My mouth boasts over my enemies,*
> *for I delight in your deliverance.*

"There is no one holy like the Lord;
there is no one besides you;
there is no Rock like our God."

1 Samuel 2:1-2

Hannah's prayer may well have spontaneously come to Mary's mind. As Jon Sweeney writes, "Hannah … prefigures Mary. Hannah offered her first son, Samuel, to God to work in the temple, while Mary gave her only son, Jesus, as the new temple."[13] The Magnificat remains her song of praise treasured by Christians throughout the world. Just how literally her words have been preserved is not the point. It is her magnificent awareness and thanksgiving that is the message.

And Mary said:

"My soul glorifies the Lord
and my spirit rejoices in God my Savior,
for he has been mindful
of the humble state of his servant.
From now on all generations will call me blessed,
for the Mighty One has done great things for me—
holy is his name.
His mercy extends to those who fear him,
from generation to generation.
He has performed mighty deeds with his arm;
he has scattered those who are proud in their
inmost thoughts.
He has brought down rulers from their thrones
but has lifted up the humble.
He has filled the hungry with good things,
but has sent the rich away empty.
He has helped his servant Israel,
remembering to be merciful
to Abraham and his descendants forever,
even as he said to our fathers.

Luke 1:46-55

The film "Mary of Nazareth" beautifully depicts the interaction between Mary and Elizabeth.[14] Having just realized that Mary is carrying the Messiah, the Son of God, Elizabeth asks her, *"But why am I so favored that the mother of my Lord should come to me?"* Zechariah and their friends are also present. In a burst of exuberance Mary moves around the room embracing all and giving praise to God. In effect, she is singing her Magnificat. It is but one lovely interpretation of the Visitation.

So much had been happening to Mary, Elizabeth and Zechariah, and in such a short time. When Mary arrived, it would have been immediately obvious to her that Gabriel's claim of Elizabeth's pregnancy was true. Zechariah's vision in the Temple and his inability to speak (until after John was born) were additional signs for them all.

And what did Zechariah think? Long past her childbearing years, Elizabeth now carried what would be their firstborn son. Surely, he must have been awed by God's presence in their lives in such dramatic and tangible ways. And then, to be visited by young Mary and learn of her news was undoubtedly beyond anything the old priest could have envisioned. So much had happened to him in less than a year! From the Temple honor duty, to his wife's pregnancy and then Mary coming to them, to the impending birth of John. The intense spiritual moments in Zechariah's life are reflected, at least in part, in the Canticle of Zechariah, discussed in Appendix B.

Mary knew that what had happened to her and to Elizabeth and Zechariah was all God's will. We might wonder about the conversations that took place during the time they were together. Did Elizabeth advise Mary on what to say to Joseph and to her parents when she returned home? They must have had many conversations about being called to participate in God's plan. They could not foresee how events would unfold in the years ahead, only that John was destined for a future mission in God's service and that Jesus was the promised and long-awaited Messiah. We can imagine that Elizabeth was overjoyed in anticipation of loving and raising her son and feeling fulfilled by motherhood at last. Zechariah must also have been deeply moved at having a son so late in life. Together this elderly couple, along with Mary and her unborn son, had been chosen by God to participate in the unfolding mystery of salvation, what we might call a joyous mystery.

Mary stayed with them for Elizabeth's last trimester. Did she remain with them for the circumcision of their son? Probably not. Luke tells us first that *"Mary stayed with Elizabeth for about three months and then returned home"* (Luke 1:56). Then he tells us of the birth and circumcision of John. He seems to emphasize that Mary's primary alliance was with her own family rather than with her cousin's family. Thus, she should depart before the birth of John and his circumcision. It was important to Luke to indicate the primacy of Jesus.

When Mary headed for home, she faced a challenge. She knew the Jewish laws and customs by which they all lived. According to Jewish law, during their betrothal Joseph could divorce Mary. She was also opening herself to condemnation and punishment from the community, even the possibility of death by stoning under a presumption of adultery. Knowing this, why didn't she stay with Elizabeth and Zechariah? She might have been safer in Zechariah's priestly household, under his protection. But after staying there for just three months, she returned to Nazareth, in a supreme demonstration of faith, trust and courage.

It goes deeper than that. Mary certainly knew that difficulties lay ahead. But she also knew with absolute certainty that she was loved by God, and that she had been given a sacred task. She may have felt an inner compulsion to return home to her family and to Joseph, even though she may not have known how they would receive her.

Hopefully we, too, know we are loved by God. Some of us may say as much. But when difficulties arise, we may find it hard to believe he really does love us. Fr. Ronald Rolheiser, O.M.I., has observed that when we fail at something or our world turns dark, we find it difficult to believe that God could still love us.[15] For example, I have volunteered in the Kairos Prison Ministry where there is often a feeling among the prisoners that God could not love them because of what they have done in the past. The prisoners have great difficulty forgiving themselves and others and an even greater difficulty in coming to believe they are worthy of God's forgiveness and love. But when they do discover God's love, mercy and forgiveness a new world opens for them. More than one prisoner has told me, "I may be here for life, but now I'm free!"

Mary knew deep in her soul that she was loved by God. She fully accepted and returned his love. Her knowledge gave her the trust and courage she needed to return to her village and let events unfold. As St. Paul wrote, *"If God is for us, who can be against us?"* (Romans 8:31). Would any of us have had such faith and trust? Trust in God is embedded within faith. They go together, reinforcing each other through life. Mary could be faithful because she knew and trusted that God would always be lovingly faithful to her. Mary is our model of openness to God's love and of the way to live with faith, trust and love.

Her first trimester over, Mary awaited the next six months and the fulfillment of God's promise to her. Yet during the same time, her relationship with Joseph, her parents and others had to be resolved.

Thoughts to Ponder

- Elizabeth and Mary were both women of destiny. Elizabeth's son John would grow up to serve the Lord and to baptize the Son of God, whose sandals he felt unworthy to loosen. He accepted and lived his vocation. Mary likewise accepted and lived her vocation to bear and care for the Messiah. What do you accept as your vocation?

- It is often said that our God is a God of surprises. Sarah, Hannah and Elizabeth were all surprised to become pregnant long after they had given up hope of having children. Have you experienced any of God's surprises in your life? How did you respond to them?

- Perhaps we gloss over the fact that Elizabeth so readily recognized Mary as *the mother of (her) Lord.* Elizabeth was a faith-filled person graced by God. Luke tells us that she was filled with the Holy Spirit at the very moment when she and Mary met. How do you recognize the promptings of the Holy Spirit in your life? How do you act on them?

- On one level, religion can be easy: join a church, learn its teachings and participate in its services. But faith goes beyond simple church membership. The purpose of the Church is to teach the truth of the Good News and to facilitate a personal relationship with Jesus in each of us. The responsibility for that relationship belongs to us individually, and it requires both trust and faith. Without trust, faith remains immature. What is your feeling about this?

- Mary was graced by God in very special and unique ways. We, too, in less dramatic ways, can receive God's grace! Have you experienced or been aware of moments of grace in your life?

Chapter Four

The Nativity

"But you, Bethlehem Ephrathah,* though you are small among the clans of Judah, out of you will come for me one who will be ruler over Israel, whose origins are from of old, from ancient times."

Micah 5:2

In order that Christ's body might be shown to be a real body, He was born of a woman; in order that His Godhead might be made clear, He was born of a virgin.

St. Thomas Aquinas[16]

From the Gospels of Matthew and Luke

The birth of Jesus is related in the Gospels of Matthew and Luke. Both writers relate that Mary became pregnant by the Holy Spirit

---

* Ephrathah: an ancient name for Bethlehem or the area which included Bethlehem.

while betrothed to Joseph. Both also report that she later gave birth in Bethlehem, to a son named Jesus. In other respects, the two narratives are quite different, leaving us much to consider.

As we discussed in earlier chapters, Luke begins his Gospel with accounts of events that took place prior to Jesus' birth, including the miraculous pregnancy of Mary's cousin Elizabeth, Gabriel's announcement to Mary that she would bear the son of God, Mary's visit to Elizabeth and the birth of John the Baptist. Matthew does not discuss any of these events. Instead, he begins his Gospel with a genealogy showing Jesus' descent from Abraham, after which he proceeds almost directly to Jesus' birth.

The genealogy Matthew presents is important because he was writing for a Jewish audience and wanted to show them how Jesus descended from an honored ancestral line. Beginning with Abraham, he traces Jesus' ancestry down through the generations, naming many key figures in Jewish history, most notably King David, and ending with *"Jacob the father of Joseph, the husband of Mary, of whom was born Jesus, who is called Christ"* (Matthew 1:16). Matthew thus makes it clear that Mary was Jesus' biological mother while Joseph was his father in the legal sense.

The genealogy is interesting for another reason. Five women are included in the list: Tamar, Rahab, Ruth, Bathsheba (by inference) and Mary, the first three of whom were Gentiles. In this way Matthew showed his audience that Jesus was of and for all humankind, both men and women, Jew and Gentile.

Luke recounts how Mary returned home to Nazareth after visiting Elizabeth for three months (Luke 1:56), which would mean that she was about three months pregnant at that point. It is doubtful that she was showing. But as the weeks went by and her condition became evident, we can only wonder at what the villagers were thinking and perhaps gossiping about her. What did Mary tell Joseph and how did he respond? In their paternalistic society, how was Mary's father Joachim responding? Was Mary being shunned? We know nothing of the conversations between Mary and Joseph, or between Mary and her parents. Luke and Matthew are silent about all of this.

Matthew says simply that during the time when Mary and Joseph were betrothed, Mary *"was found to be with child through the Holy Spirit"* (Matthew 1:18), and that *"because Joseph her husband was a righteous man and did not want to expose her to public disgrace, he had in mind to divorce her quietly"* (Matthew 1:19), thus ending their intended union.

A Jewish betrothal of marriage followed well-established customs. Normally, both sets of parents had to agree to the marriage. Mary's parents presumably had already agreed to the marriage. We are not aware of Joseph's parents being involved, or even if they were still alive at this time. Since Joseph was older than Mary and working on his own, his parents' permission may not have been necessary. A betrothal could last up to a year, during which a couple was considered married but would not yet live together or have sexual relations. It was during this time that Joseph could have divorced Mary when he became aware that she was pregnant by another.

The betrothal period had to be a most difficult time for Joseph. He evidently cared for Mary and hoped to ease her disgrace by divorcing her quietly, although it would hardly go unnoticed in the village where everyone was aware of all happenings. Perhaps in this way Mary would escape more severe punishment for her presumed adultery. It was at this time that an angel appeared to Joseph in a dream and said,

> *"Joseph son of David, do not be afraid to take Mary home as your wife, because what is conceived in her is from the Holy Spirit. She will give birth to a son, and you are to give him the name Jesus, because he will save his people from their sins."*
>
> Matthew 1:20-21

This was not an invitation such as Mary received in the Gospel of Luke, but a direct instruction! Matthew continues,

> *All this took place to fulfill what the Lord had said through the prophet: "The virgin will be with child and will give*

birth to a son, and they will call him Immanuel"—which means, "God with us." When Joseph woke up, he did what the angel of the Lord had commanded him and took Mary home as his wife.

Matthew 1:22-24

If Mary had already told him she was pregnant by the Holy Spirit, presumably now he could accept it. Just as, in Luke's Gospel, Mary said "yes" to God's invitation, Joseph, in Matthew's Gospel, said "yes" to the message of instruction he received by accepting Mary as his wife.

Matthew does not describe their wedding, but in a traditional Jewish wedding the community would be invited to witness the marriage ceremony, with the couple standing beneath a *chuppah*. A *chuppah* is a cloth canopy supported by four poles. It symbolizes the home and life the couple will soon build together. The groom enters first, followed by the bride, signifying the taking of his bride into his home.

Matthew tells us that although Joseph took Mary home as his wife, "he had no union with her until she gave birth to a son" (Matthew 1:25).

Joseph could now assume the roles of husband, father, provider and protector. In their community he would be assumed and accepted to be the child's father. Joseph's role as husband to Mary and father to Jesus would make life as secure as possible for his wife and child. His presence would provide a social shield for Mary. She was now married to a respectable, hardworking man. She and her baby would be safe in their community.

What do we know of the man Joseph? He was the son of Jacob and descended from the line of David (Matthew 1:16). We know little of his father, Jacob. Jacob is assumed to have been a carpenter because sons typically learned their fathers' trades. For the same reason we can assume that Joseph taught these skills in turn to Jesus. Matthew tells us that after Jesus began his public ministry and was performing miracles people would exclaim, *"Isn't this the carpenter's son?"* (Matthew

13:55). Being a carpenter, Joseph probably did various jobs as a construction worker, which may explain why he lived in Nazareth close to the growing commercial town of Sepphoris, where carpentry and construction work would have been more readily available.

I suspect many of us grew up with the impression that Joseph was old. Scripture is silent about his age, so how did the idea originate? The canon of the Bible was affirmed and codified during the Council of Trent, 1545 to 1563. Well before that time many writings appeared in addition to those ultimately accepted into the Bible. The apocryphal Gospel of James was one. Scholars date it to between 178 and 204 A.D. In other words, it was written well after the texts attributed to Matthew, Mark, Luke, John, Paul and others in the New Testament. It purports to tell the story of Mary and of Jesus' birth, but has been discredited as of questionable authenticity on many issues. However, in its time it was widely circulated and led to the popular belief that Joseph was an old widower. In one passage that describes the selection of a husband for Mary, it states, "But Joseph objected [to the high priest], 'I already have sons and I'm an old man; she's only a young woman. I'm afraid that I'll become the butt of jokes among the people of Israel.'"[17] This and other passages gave rise to the belief that Mary's virginity would be protected by Joseph because, as an elderly man, he was supposedly no longer virile. This belief was supported and strengthened by many painters, particularly European artists from the fifteenth to seventeenth centuries.[18] It was thought that if Joseph was seen as an old man, it would be easier to accept Mary as ever-virgin. For example, a detail of the larger painting *The Mystic Nativity* by Sandro Botticelli (1446-1510) depicts Joseph as mostly bald with a fringe of gray hair, hunched down and looking quite old in marked contrast to the much younger Mary.

By the early nineteenth century, perceptions began to change. In *The Carpenter's Shop*, a painting by British artist John Everett Millais (1829-1896), Joseph is at his carpentry bench. He looks strong and perhaps in his thirties or early forties. He is clearly not elderly. Young Jesus appears to be around six or seven and has wounded his hand on a nail. Mary kisses him and Joseph examines the wound. Jesus' grandmother, Anne, points to the nail on the table.

The Mystic Nativity (detail) by Sandro Botticelli
Photograph courtesy of The National Gallery, London

Christ in the House of his Parents (The Carpenter's Shop)
by John Everett Millais
Courtesy of the Tate Gallery, London

Joseph was undoubtedly older than Mary. That was normal for the place and time. Joseph accepted Jesus with love, protected him and, with Mary, raised him to adulthood. God blessed Joseph with physical, moral and spiritual strength to protect his family. As Fulton J. Sheen writes,

> To make Joseph out as old portrays for us a man who had little vital energy left, rather than one who, having it, kept it in chains for God's sake and for His holy purposes. To make Joseph appear pure only because his flesh had aged is like glorifying a mountain stream that has dried.[19]

We accept Mary's strength to do God's will, but we sometimes forget Joseph's faith and obedience to do God's will as well.

Matthew says little about the birth of Jesus. He simply states, *"After Jesus was born in Bethlehem in Judea, during the time of King Herod, Magi from the east came to Jerusalem"* (Matthew 2:1). He gives no explanation for how or why Jesus was born in Bethlehem, and no indication that the Holy Family lived in Nazareth prior to that. Reading only his Gospel, one would have no idea why they were there. For that we must return to Luke, who gives a more detailed account of Jesus' birth. He tells us,

> *In those days Caesar Augustus issued a decree that a census should be taken of the entire Roman world. (This was the first census that took place while Quirinius was governor of Syria.) And everyone went to his own town to register.*
>
> Luke 2:1-3

Scholars and theologians agree that there is no historical evidence that the Roman emperor issued such a decree or that the census actually occurred. However, Luke was intent on placing Mary and Joseph in Bethlehem for the birth. The census may be a literary device to justify the journey from Nazareth to Bethlehem. Joseph would have had to go to Bethlehem, "*the town of David, because he belonged to the house and line of David*" (Luke 2:4). In any case, Luke and Matthew agree on the birth of Jesus occurring in Bethlehem.

In Luke's account, although Mary's baby was nearly due, she traveled with Joseph to Bethlehem. Did she have to go, or could she have stayed behind until her baby was born? One wonders if Mary's mother tried to persuade her to stay in Nazareth where she would have family and perhaps a trusted midwife to help with the birth. We can infer, however, that Mary chose to accompany Joseph to Bethlehem. It is an intriguing issue because Mary may have been aware of this passage in Micah: "*But you, Bethlehem Ephrathah, though you are small among the clans of Judah, out of you will come for me one who will be ruler over Israel, whose origins are from old, from ancient times*" (Micah 5:2). It was revealed to Mary at the Annunciation that she would give birth to the Son of God. Micah foretold that the "ruler," the Messiah, would come from Bethlehem in Judea, the birthplace of King David. If Mary was aware of this prophecy, it may have reinforced her desire to accompany Joseph instead of remaining in Nazareth. Or did she simply need to be with her husband under his care and protection? Perhaps the desire to go with him was a guiding grace from God.

Luke says nothing of the journey from Nazareth to Bethlehem, a distance of about eighty miles. It would have taken them perhaps five days with Mary now in her ninth month. This journey is often depicted in art, with Mary riding a donkey. That is quite plausible since they would also need to carry clothing, food and Joseph's tools. It must have been uncomfortable for Mary with a baby nearly due, suffering the plodding gait of an animal. Undoubtedly, she would walk when she could. Tiresome as the journey may have been, they eventually arrived in Bethlehem.

Luke states that, "*While they were there, the time came for the baby to be born, and she gave birth to her firstborn, a son. She wrapped him in cloths and placed him in a manger, because there was no room for them in the inn*" (Luke 2:6-7). How very poignant! She gave birth to the Messiah, yet the world had nothing to give him but a cave, some straw and an animal trough for a bed.

Shortly after the birth, Luke says that an angel appeared to shepherds in nearby fields and told them, *"Today in the town of David a Savior has been born to you; he is Christ the Lord"* (Luke 2:11). This was an early sign that Jesus had come into the world for all humankind. He continues, *"Suddenly a great company of the heavenly host appeared with the angel, praising God and saying, 'Glory to God in the highest, and on earth peace to men on whom his favor rests'"* (Luke 2:13-14).

This incident is remarkable because at that time, shepherds were considered to be among the lowest members of society. Yet God chose them to be his early evangelists: *"When they had seen him, they spread the word concerning what had been told them about this child, and all who heard it were amazed at what the shepherds said to them"* (Luke 2:17-18). For her part, Luke says that *"Mary treasured up all these things and pondered them in her heart"* (Luke 2:19).

I can picture Mary holding her newborn son, gazing at him with unconditional love, kissing and nursing him. I like to think of Joseph watching over them, awed by the miracle that he was chosen by God to protect. It recalls to my mind a moment in my own family's lives. My daughter Kathe held her baby Megan and then gently placed her on a blanket by the warmth of the fireplace. As she knelt by her baby, she looked at her with such complete love that she was transfixed. Her face was glowing with inexpressible joy, love and awe. I was sitting nearby, deeply moved by the unconditional love I was privileged to witness. Precious new life does that for us. Families privileged to receive a newborn baby participate in the miracle of God's love in a way that cannot be adequately described.

Over the centuries, some have tried to explain how the incarnate Christ came into the world, giving rise to fanciful stories about how Jesus wasn't born in the usual way, but simply appeared.[20] It seems far better to honor Mary's humanity by accepting that her child, conceived by the Holy Spirit and nurtured in her womb, experienced a perfectly natural birth. As St. Thomas Aquinas (1225-1274) wrote,

"In order that Christ's body might be shown to be a real body, He was born of a woman. In order that His Godhead might be made clear, He was born of a virgin."[21]

There is an old saying, "A baby is God's proof that there will be a tomorrow." With the birth of Jesus, the world's tomorrows would be forever transformed, yet in the eyes of the world at that time, Mary and Joseph were people of no importance.

In Luke's account, the circumcision and Presentation of Jesus in the Temple occurred next, but they are of such importance that they will be treated separately, in Chapter 5. Matthew's story of the Magi took place even later, just prior to the Holy Family's flight into Egypt. Accordingly, the Magi will be discussed in Chapter 6.

Thoughts to Ponder

- Luke writes of the shepherds but makes no mention of Magi. Matthew writes of the Magi but says nothing of shepherds. Two narratives, similar in some ways but differing in important details. How do you account for such differences between the Gospel accounts and do they disturb you?

- Over time we have romanticized portions of our Christian faith story. Would Mary and Joseph recognize our telling of the Christmas story today? Do we understand the Nativity story as it truly was, or do we gloss over the challenges that Mary and Joseph faced to bring the Messiah into the world? What do their struggles mean to your faith today?

- A modern Christian sacramental marriage is not much different from marriage in Mary and Joseph's time. Then as now, there was an engagement period followed by a wedding ceremony conducted by a priest, with family and friends witnessing. In our culture, parents do not arrange a union for their daughters and sons, but they do give the couple their blessing and support. Is liturgical marriage important to you, as it was in Mary and Joseph's day? Why or why not?

- Do we take to mind and heart that the story of Christ's nativity was lived out for our benefit? What lessons can we learn from the Holy Family at Jesus' birth? What is the most meaningful part of the story to you?

- Author Mark Miravalle shows us how fundamental the incarnation is for all of salvation history: "If you don't have the Nativity, you don't have Calvary, and if you don't have Calvary, you don't have Redemption."[22] The Annunciation and the birth of Jesus were the beginning of a new covenant of salvation through Christ Jesus. This is the joyous mystery of God's love for humankind. Jesus became man while remaining truly God. How do you comprehend the two natures, human and divine, of Jesus?

Chapter Five

The Presentation in the Temple

*The Lord said to Moses, "Consecrate to me every firstborn
male. The firstborn offspring of every womb among the
Israelites belongs to me, whether man or animal."*

Exodus 13:1-2

*When the time of their purification according to the Law of Moses
had been completed, Joseph and Mary took him to Jerusalem to
present him to the Lord (as it is written in the Law of the Lord,
"Every firstborn male is to be consecrated to the Lord.")*

Luke 2:22-23

From the Gospel of Luke

Jesus' circumcision followed eight days after his birth, according to
the Law of Moses. At his circumcision, *"he was named Jesus, the name
the angel had given him before he had been conceived"* (Luke 2:21).

The name is a Greek version of the Hebrew name Yeshua, meaning "the Lord saves." This is what both Mary and Joseph had been told to name the child (in Luke and Matthew, respectively), *"because,"* as explained to Joseph, *"he will save his people from their sins"* (Matthew 1:21). Luke does not say where the circumcision took place. Perhaps it was performed in Bethlehem by a local rabbi and witnessed by Joseph's relatives. Most likely, a celebratory party would then have concluded the event. Some weeks later, Mary and Joseph went to the Temple in Jerusalem to present their son to God. In obedience to the Law of Moses, Mary first waited the prescribed forty days for her purification to be completed. Mary, like all women who had just given birth, was precluded from public worship until declared ritually clean. For mothers of sons this period was seven days from birth to circumcision and thirty-three days thereafter, for a total of forty days (Leviticus 12:1-4).

Mary, chosen by God, graced with bearing the incarnate Christ, nevertheless was subject to the Law of Moses just like all other Israelites. Despite her specialness we must always remember her humanness. Mary lived within the structures and discipline of her Jewish faith. She and Joseph would never have considered living outside that faith and its teachings.

From Bethlehem to Jerusalem was a distance of five or six miles, an easy walk for them. Old Jerusalem was a walled city. Inside the city walls was the Temple, surrounded by its own massive wall. The Temple had a large area called the Court of the Gentiles which was open to all. Merchants sold animals for sacrifice there and money changers exchanged currency. Roman coins were not accepted for payment in the Temple. To accommodate this, money changers would convert Roman coins to Jewish shekels. Access to the Temple itself was strictly controlled by priests. Women were forbidden from entering certain areas, including the Court of the Priests, the Sanctuary and the Holy of Holies. They were allowed in the Court of the Women, an outer forecourt, which is where Mary would have presented herself to a priest to be declared ritually clean and to receive his blessing. Joseph would have accompanied her, perhaps holding Jesus, but standing aside. Following the purification ritual, they would have made a prescribed sacrificial offering, after which they could then present their son to God.

Luke's reference to Jesus as a firstborn son is important, but it does not mean Mary had other children later on. It is drawn directly from the Book of Exodus: *"The Lord said to Moses, 'Consecrate to me every firstborn male. The first offspring of every womb among the Israelites belongs to me, whether man or animal'"* (Exodus 13:1-2). This theme is repeated throughout the Old Testament, and in the New Testament it is affirmed by Luke (2:22-23).

While in the Temple area, Mary and Joseph were approached by an elderly man named Simeon. We know little about Simeon except that he was *"righteous and devout"* (Luke 2:25) and that the Holy Spirit had revealed to him that he would not die before seeing the Messiah (Luke 2:25-26). The apocryphal James describes him as a priest.[23] Luke does not. My belief is that he was a layman. Just at the time that Mary and Joseph brought Jesus to the Temple, Simeon was inspired, indeed moved, by the Holy Spirit to come see them.

Simeon took the baby in his arms. Filled with insight and emotion, he said,

> *"Sovereign Lord, as you have promised,*
> *you now dismiss your servant in peace.*
> *For my eyes have seen your salvation,*
> *which you have prepared in the sight of all people,*
> *a light for revelation to the Gentiles*
> *and for glory to your people Israel."*
>
> Luke 2:29-32

What a moment that must have been for the little party! Simeon was overcome with joy and thanksgiving at seeing and acknowledging the promised Messiah. Luke adds, *"The child's father and mother marveled at what was said about him"* (Luke 2:33).

Notice the phrase, *"a light for revelation to the Gentiles and for glory to your people Israel."* The statement is an indication that the long-awaited Messiah was coming for all people and not just for the chosen people of Israel. This theme is repeated in Matthew when the Magi, who were Gentiles, came to worship Jesus (Matthew 2:1-12, discussed in the next chapter). The Israelites had understandably believed that the Messiah would come for them exclusively, considering their covenant with Yahweh. So these passages indicate a broadening of the understanding of the Messiah and his purpose.

After blessing them, Simeon then said to Mary, *"This child is destined to cause the falling and rising of many in Israel, and to be a sign that will be spoken against, so that the thoughts of many hearts will be revealed"* (Luke 2:34-35). Considering the import of Simeon's message to Mary, we can imagine that he may have paused, and then looking directly into her eyes, said, *"And a sword will pierce your own soul too"* (Luke 2:35).

What was Mary to make of these words? The Presentation in the Temple was meant to be a moment of happiness for Mary and Joseph. Their healthy child had been blessed, given back to them and recognized by Simeon for who he truly was, the Messiah. Yet the word "too" suggests that both Mary and her precious son would suffer. We often read that Mary kept these things in her heart and pondered over them. Of course she did, and we can assume Joseph did as well. It would be natural for Mary and Joseph to discuss all events that had such an impact on their lives. Simeon was an old man, one to be highly respected in their culture and obviously devoted to God. Mary and Joseph would have listened to him with respect and most likely with awe. What he said was unexpected, puzzling and fearsome all at the same time.

Why would Simeon say that to Mary? Did the Holy Spirit give him foresight into the suffering of Christ? His prayer, referred to as Nunc Dimittis ("now dismiss" in the Latin version), is testimony to his faith and openness to the Holy Spirit. His prophetic warning was not idle talk. This was a serious message for Mary.

Then an old prophetess, Anna, who never left the Temple, came up to them and *"gave thanks to God and spoke about the child to all who were looking forward to the redemption of Jerusalem"* (Luke 2:38).

The list of those blessed with the grace to recognize the baby as the Messiah was continuing to grow. Not only did Anna recognize Jesus for who he was, but she went about proclaiming the news in the Temple. One wonders how the news was received by the Temple priests. Perhaps they just ignored her.

Passing lightly over the Presentation itself, Luke then tells us, *"When Joseph and Mary had done everything required by the Law of the Lord, they returned to Galilee to their own town of Nazareth"* (Luke 2:39). In reading Luke, one may wonder which came first, the meetings with Simeon and Anna or the Presentation? On this point Luke is not very clear and one could interpret the flow of events either way. I have elected to place the meetings with Simeon and Anna first, since Luke describes them in some detail whereas he glosses over the Presentation.

For the Presentation of Jesus, his parents would have needed to purchase a sacrificial animal such as an unblemished lamb. However, a lamb would have been beyond their means. The Law of Moses allowed people of lesser means to purchase a pair of birds to satisfy Temple requirements. Mary and Joseph were subject to and faithful to the Law of Moses as detailed in Leviticus. Accordingly, they bought *"a pair of doves or two young pigeons"* (Luke 2:24). In the Court of Women, they would have presented their two birds for the ritual sacrifice. The parents would then, with a Temple priest, offer their child to God, dedicating him to serve God throughout his life. The sacrifice of birds ritually represented a blood offering. Think of Abraham offering to sacrifice his beloved son, Isaac. Just as God spared Isaac and returned him to Abraham, the priest would then return the child to his parents. As Mary and Joseph received their child back, they both knew something of the larger truth of Jesus' destiny. With the Presentation in the Temple now complete, they could contemplate the next phase of their family life.

In the days ahead, Mary must have thought over Simeon's prophecy and prayed for understanding and acceptance. What else could she do but pray and meet each new day as it presented itself? Mary was never a complainer, but faithful to God's will as well as she could discern it. Mary and Joseph show us that faith is a step beyond simply believing what you can see. It includes trust. It is accepting that which cannot be seen. In other words, *"Now faith is being sure of what we hope for and certain of what we do not see"* (Hebrews 11:1).

As we consider the Presentation of Jesus in the Temple, I am reminded of an incident I witnessed on a Cursillo retreat at Whispering Winds Catholic Camp near Julian, California. About a hundred men took part in the retreat. An altar had been set up under a huge oak tree and Fr. Walter Vogel, O.S.A., was preparing to celebrate Mass. A few other guests were invited because there was to be a baptism. Fr. Walt called the baby's parents, Jim and Teresa, forward to present their son. He explained to the community gathered that Danny was a miracle baby born of faith, hope, love and much prayer. For many years Jim and Teresa had longed for a child. Their prayers were finally answered with a beautiful and healthy baby boy.

Following Danny's baptism, Fr. Walt handed him back to his father. Jim then walked with his son up and down the rows of men so that this gift from God could be welcomed into the community by each of them. Until then a man in the back row seemed to have been unaffected by the retreat. But when Jim approached him and offered Danny to him for a blessing, he broke down. God's love in the form of this innocent baby touched his heart in a way that no one else had been able to do. Later, following the Liturgy of the Word, Fr. Walt raised Danny high above the altar, offering Jim and Teresa's firstborn son to God before returning him to his parents. The ritual has spiritual meaning and value today just as it did in Mary and Joseph's time.

It is interesting that in his Gospel, Luke then has the Holy Family returning directly to Nazareth in Galilee, making no mention of the Magi, the family's flight into Egypt, or the Slaughter of the Innocents. For that portion of the story we will return to Matthew's Gospel.

Thoughts to Ponder

- Jesus is consubstantial with the Father and the Holy Spirit. Yet he was taken to the Temple to be presented to God. Why was the Presentation necessary? What does it tell us about Jesus' active participation in our human society?

- Truth reveals itself slowly as we age and gain experience. How much more so it must have seemed to Mary and Joseph. Graced in so many ways, they still had to trust in the mysteries laid before them, understanding some happenings in their lives while being perplexed and even frightened by others. Is this not true for all of us as we live our lives? How has God surprised or challenged you?

- Simeon was likely not a Temple priest, but rather a devout layman with an unshakable belief that he would see the Messiah before he died. Was he expecting the Messiah as a baby or as others pictured him, a warrior king like David, ready to defeat the Romans and free the Israelites? Do our own preconceived and culturally shaped notions sometimes blind us to the truth as it unfolds before us? What spiritual understandings have changed for you over time?

- Wisdom comes to the elderly from a lifetime of experiences and reflections. So it was with Simeon and Anna. In their culture, as in many cultures around the world, elders were revered for their life wisdom, and younger generations learned and benefited from them. How well do we accept the gifts of wisdom from the elderly today?

Chapter Six

The Magi, Herod and the Flight into Egypt

*"A voice is heard in Ramah, mourning and great weeping,
Rachel weeping for her children and refusing to be
comforted, because her children are no more."*

Jeremiah 31:15

*An angel of the Lord appeared to Joseph in a dream. "Get up," he
said, "take the child and his mother and escape to Egypt. Stay there
until I tell you, for Herod is going to search for the child to kill him."*

Matthew 2:13

From the Gospel of Matthew

Following the Presentation in the Temple as described by Luke, Mary
and Joseph could now begin to consider their next plans. Their first

responsibility, as with all parents, was the care and protection of their child. Jesus was safe with them and the rituals required by the Law of Moses had been completed. Matthew now relates very different information about the Holy Family.

But first, consider the literary focus Matthew uses to tell his story and why. A strategy he consistently uses is to connect the narrative about Jesus and his family to ancient Scriptures, in particular to Old Testament prophecies. For example, he says that when Jesus and his family left Egypt, it was in fulfillment of a prophecy in Hosea: *"When Israel was a child, I loved him, and out of Egypt I called my son"* (Hosea 11:1 and Matthew 2:15).

Matthew also aims to show that the divine power of Jesus will ultimately prove superior to the temporal power of kings. In the meantime, the child Jesus must be kept safe until, as an adult, he can fulfill his mission.

Matthew also blends historical facts with literary devices. For example, King Herod and his successor, Archelaus, were historical figures, as recorded by the historian Josephus, whereas the Slaughter of the Innocents and the flight into Egypt are not historical events. The Gospels were not intended as history in the modern sense of that word. Instead, they tell the inspired truth that the incarnate Christ was born into the world to bring God's plan of salvation forward. The four evangelists expressed this fundamental truth in their own ways, leading to differences in their narratives, although they all agree that Jesus was the Messiah.

As mentioned in Chapter 4, Matthew says little about Jesus' birth. But he describes in detail a visit by *"Magi from the east"* some months after the birth of Jesus, which he says occurred during the reign of King Herod the Great (Matthew 2:1). Unfortunately, we are accustomed to the Christmas story depicting the Magi arriving to pay homage to Jesus just after the arrival of the shepherds. But as the NIV Biblical footnote to Matthew 2:11 explains, "Contrary to tradition, the Magi did not visit Jesus at the manger on the night of his birth as did the shepherds. They came some months later and visited him as a 'child' in his 'house.'"

Also, despite the beautiful Christmas carol, "We Three Kings of Orient Are," the Magi were not kings, although they were likely highborn, wealthy persons, respected astrologers or perhaps magicians. Tradition holds that there were three and has even given them names: Melchior, Balthasar and Gaspar. But there is no biblical evidence for their names or even that there were three.

The Magi arrived first in Jerusalem, where they asked, *"Where is the one who has been born King of the Jews? We saw his star in the east and have come to worship him"* (Matthew 2:2). Matthew describes the star as moving westward ahead of the Magi and stopping *"over the place where the child was"* (Matthew 2:9). Astronomers have tried diligently to confirm any celestial event from that time that could be interpreted as such a "star," but to no avail.[24] However, the image of a star leading respected Gentiles to find and worship the new King of the Jews enhances Matthew's narrative and broadens the understanding of who the Messiah was coming for. Such an image would have been accepted by people of that time. It was generally thought that when a new king was anointed a special star would appear.

Herod felt threatened by the Magi's report and what it implied concerning his grip on power, but he seems to have been only dimly aware of the prophecy concerning the Messiah. He called together the chief priests and lawyers and asked where the Messiah was to be born.

> *"In Bethlehem in Judea,"* they replied, *"for this is what
> the prophet has written:*
> *"'But you, Bethlehem, in the land of Judah,*
> *   are by no means least among the rulers of Judah;*
> *for out of you will come a ruler*
> *   who will be the shepherd of my people Israel.'"*
>   Matthew 2:5-6 and Micah 5:2

Herod then engages the Magi directly: *"Herod called the Magi secretly and found out from them the exact time the star had appeared"* (Matthew 2:7). He sent them on to Bethlehem with instructions to return: *"As soon as you find him, report to me, so that I too may go and worship him" (Matthew 2:8).* Bethlehem is only about five miles from Jerusalem, so the last leg of their journey would be a short one. One wonders why Herod's agents did not simply follow them! Perhaps Herod could not conceive of the Magi disobeying him.

The Magi then followed the star to the house of Mary and Joseph in Bethlehem, where they *"bowed down and worshiped him ... and presented him with gifts of gold and of incense and of myrrh"* (Matthew 2:11); hence the tradition of three Magi: one for each gift. Biblical scholar William Barclay explains, "Gold for a king, frankincense for a priest, myrrh for one who was to die."[25]

Then we read that, *"having been warned in a dream not to go back to Herod, they returned to their country by another route"* (Matthew 2:12). They had encountered the living Christ. Were they changed, as perhaps all are who encounter Jesus?

The fact that the Magi came from the east (perhaps Persia or Arabia) and that they were aware of the Messianic prophecy and searching for its fulfillment must have been more than enough to concern Herod. Obsessed with power, any perceived threat to that power would enrage him. He had learned that the child must be in Bethlehem. He perceived that if the child lived, his reign might eventually be threatened. The Jewish people knew, believed and cherished the prophecy of the coming of a King of the Jews. Embodied in their beliefs at that time was the expectation that they would also be freed from the yoke of the Roman rulers, on whom Herod's power depended.

No one knew when the coming of the Messiah would occur. If the people began to believe that it was occurring during Herod's reign, the result for him could be dangerous, perhaps catastrophic. As Matthew says, *"When King Herod heard this he was disturbed, and all Jerusalem with him"* (Matthew 2:3). People would become increasingly restless and it might even lead to a revolt. Could a child cause this? Herod soon reacted with unconscionable brutality. Previously, he had ruthlessly killed his wife, three sons and three other relatives as well as anyone who he thought opposed him. Herod gave orders that all male children two years old or younger in Bethlehem and the surrounding area should be killed, reasoning that one of them would be this "King of the Jews." Bethlehem was a small village, so the number of boys under the age of two would be limited, but their loss would be tragic all the same. Thus began the Slaughter of the Innocents, as the story has come to be known. How paradoxical it seems that Herod the Great, with near absolute power, would feel threatened by a child. Roman earthly power contrasted against divine power!

In a dream, Joseph was warned by an angel and told to take action: *"Get up ... take the child and his mother and escape to Egypt. Stay there until I tell you, for Herod is going to search for the child to kill him"* (Matthew 2:13). It is interesting to note that in Luke, angels speak to people directly but in Matthew they speak through dreams. Megan McKenna in her beautiful book, *Mary: Shadow of Grace*, writes,

> Many in the Jewish community refer to dreams as the forgotten language of God. Dreams, especially in Jewish understanding, are a way of communicating God's will to individuals. Jewish people are willing to stake their life on the knowledge that is given in a dream, even though they are unable to explain why they act as they do to others. They dream, and the dream becomes knowledge born of hope, faith, and belief in God.[26]

Joseph did not question the warning or hesitate. He immediately woke Mary. This is the second time he said "yes" to the Lord under mysterious circumstances. They quickly gathered Jesus and their meager belongings and silently disappeared into the night. Joseph was a decisive, vigilant man of action and of faith. When he received God's message, he listened, trusted and responded. Surely Joseph must have related his dream to Mary as they fled. Such was the bond between them that they responded as one and shared as one. But the three of them were now alone. Was it a moonlit night to help them find their way? Would Herod's soldiers come charging after them? It is unlikely at this time that Joseph and Mary knew the full horror of the unfolding massacre. But bad news travels fast! Soon enough they would have heard what was happening back in Bethlehem and why.

What anguish Mary must have felt for all those mothers and their murdered children. And the thought that Herod was seeking her own child to kill must have been horrifying. King Herod had total power over their lives. They would be defenseless against him. Would their lives always be in danger? Would innocent people suffer because of them, because of their child, Jesus? Mary must have understood that despite the evil perpetrated by Herod, Jesus had been saved for a divine purpose. He was the long-awaited Messiah, but for now he was just a child. The responsibility she and Joseph shared was enormous and must have been daunting considering the sometimes violent world they lived in.

The distance from Bethlehem to Egypt and the Nile Delta area is over two hundred miles. The fleeing family probably found their way to the well-traveled coastal trade route, the Via Maris. Perhaps by daybreak they joined with other travelers on the road. Despite the many pictures and Christmas card images of the Holy Family traveling alone it certainly would have been too dangerous for them to do so. Trader caravans might have allowed the little family to travel with them for greater mutual safety.

What must Mary and Joseph have been thinking as they traveled to a land and people they had never seen? Egypt was the land where their ancestors had been enslaved for four hundred years! Would they be safe in this foreign land? As immigrants would they be welcomed or shunned? Would Joseph be able to find work? Upon leaving Bethlehem and traveling on foot, or perhaps with a donkey, they could only go ten or fifteen miles on a good day. Traveling with a child less than two years old would certainly have slowed them down, especially with Mary nursing. At the time, mothers often nursed their children for two or three years or more. Joseph had to secure food and water for the family. Indeed, if they traveled with a group of traders along the way could they keep up the pace? At night did they sleep by the trailside? Were they able to find some better shelters along the way? How many days and nights did their journey take?

The flight into Egypt is mentioned only in Matthew's Gospel, and he says very little about this period in their lives. Where did this immigrant family settle upon arriving in Egypt? How long did they live there? There were a number of Jewish enclaves in Egypt and perhaps they settled in one of them. Perhaps the other evangelists did not have this information or were not interested in this phase of Jesus' life. Children were treasured, but their activities were generally not considered noteworthy. And yet, the visit of the Magi, Herod's wrath, the killing of innocent children and the escape to Egypt were such dramatic and powerful events that we are left to wonder why only Matthew recorded them.

The safety of the Holy Family was most likely assured once they were settled in Egypt and integrated into a Jewish community. Jesus grew from an infant to a young boy in Egypt. To what age we do not know. Mary would do as mothers do. She would lovingly care for him. She would watch over him, encouraging his first steps, teaching him to speak, washing him, feeding him, laughing with him and watching over him as he slept. As he grew into a boy, she and Joseph would instruct him in their Jewish faith. His young human nature had to be nurtured. His divine nature would emerge as he matured. Was Mary a bit surprised as he began to learn so quickly? What of his playmates? One wonders who they were and what effect playing, unawares, with the Son of God might have had on their lives.

During this time Joseph had to provide for his family. Finding work, even as a skilled craftsman, would not be easy in a land filled with native craftsmen. Joseph, an immigrant, might have been viewed with suspicion. On the other hand, if they were welcomed into a Jewish enclave, he might have found opportunities for work there. Hospitality to the Jewish stranger was embedded in their culture. In addition to his work skills, Joseph also had the gifts of gold, frankincense and myrrh with which to barter for their necessities. God does provide!

Did Herod believe, because of the massacre, that the baby rumored to be the "King of the Jews" had been killed? One wonders if he ever discovered that the Holy Family had escaped. During this period,

Herod became increasingly unhinged. Josephus, a Jewish historian of the time, labeled his condition an "incurable distemper."[27] King Herod the Great, ruler over Judea, Galilee, Iturea and Trachonitis, died in 4 B.C. Who would replace him? What would this new ruler be like? Would he be better or worse for the people he ruled over?

"After Herod died, an angel of the Lord appeared in a dream to Joseph in Egypt and said, 'Get up, take the child and his mother and go to the land of Israel, for those who were trying to take the child's life are dead'" (Matthew 2:19-20). Joseph did so. This is the third time that Joseph said "yes" to the Lord by obeying instructions he had received in a dream. Joseph, Mary and the young boy journeyed home to Israel. From the beginning, Joseph had exhibited every laudable attribute of husband, father and protector of his family, and did so with humility, integrity and faithfulness. He is truly a model for all fathers.

The Old Testament prophet Hosea wrote, *"When Israel was a child, I loved him, and out of Egypt I called my son"* (Hosea 11:1). And in Matthew: *"And so was fulfilled what the Lord had said through the prophet: 'Out of Egypt I called my son'"* (Matthew 2:15). As applied by Matthew, the prophecy has a double meaning. God saved his "son," Israel, and brought him out of bondage in Egypt. So, also, God saved his son, Jesus, and brought him out of Egypt.

On their return to Judea, Joseph learned that Archelaus, Herod's son, now ruled. Archelaus proved to be as evil and cruel as his father. Concerned for his family, Joseph was again warned in a dream. For their safety, he took them north to the region of Galilee and settled in Nazareth. As Matthew notes, *"So was fulfilled what was said through the prophets: 'He will be called a Nazarene'"* (Matthew 2:23). Indeed, throughout his ministry Jesus was known as a Nazarene. Is this important? Yes, names and places where one came from were important identifiers in their day. Recall how Peter was challenged by a servant girl after Jesus was arrested: *"You also were with that Nazarene, Jesus"* (Mark 14:67). And at the Resurrection, when Mary Magdalene went to the tomb a young man said to her, *"Don't be alarmed ... You are looking for Jesus the Nazarene, who was crucified. He has risen! He is not here"* (Mark 16:6).

Matthew writes of a series of events that would seem to be of great consequence: the star from the east, the visit of the Magi, the Slaughter of the Innocents and the flight into Egypt, all before the Holy Family returned to Nazareth. It is puzzling that such momentous events are only described in one Gospel. Yet there are many other examples of important events that appear in only one Gospel. For example, the Marriage Feast at Cana appears only in John's Gospel. Despite the differences between the Gospels there is one constant theme: that Jesus is the Christ, sent by the Father for the redemption and salvation of humankind. Each Gospel writer determined how best to present this truth. They did so in different ways and for different audiences. Like us, they were products of their own experiences of time and place and most profoundly by their experiences of Jesus before and after his death and resurrection. Most of us find that looking back at a major event in our lives and after some time has passed, we are able to understand its meaning more deeply. It must have been so for the four evangelists. Their Gospels were not written as history, but as sacred memories of a revealed truth that had to be shared.

Each Gospel story is to be treasured for what it has passed on to us about the life of Jesus, Mary and Joseph. Luke's and Matthew's accounts differ in important ways. But they simply chose the events that meant the most to them in telling us about Jesus—who he was, his journey with his family and the unfolding meaning of his life.

Thoughts to Ponder

- Time and again, Holy Scripture emphasizes the interaction between God and his people. Angels, God's messengers, are ever-present. Sometimes the message is inviting, as with the Annunciation. At other times, as with Joseph, it is more directive. Mary and Joseph were open and receptive to God's messages. How open and receptive are you?

- That Jesus was welcomed both by lowly Jewish shepherds and by highborn Gentiles, by Simeon and by Anna, is an indication that Jesus came for us all, not just for any one group or sect. Yet we humans are often "tribal" people. We confine ourselves to our own comfortable, self-same communities. We are shaped by our culture, the times we live in and by the geography of our place. Too often we are suspicious of others, sometimes even hostile to them. Considering Jesus' teachings and his own examples of inclusiveness, how inclusive are you toward others?

- It is easy to romanticize the Holy Family's escape into Egypt. But they were poor immigrants fleeing their homeland for the safety of their son. Families continue to do that to this day. Recently, many families fleeing violence and poverty in Central America traveled great distances to seek sanctuary in the United States, a difficult journey undertaken in the hope of safety for their children. Yet many of these children were separated and held in facilities away from their parents. Sometimes we ignore God's call for compassion and mercy toward the less fortunate, even to children in danger. How do you respond to those in need or fleeing danger?

Chapter Seven

The Holy Family in Nazareth

"Celebrate the Feast of Unleavened Bread; for seven days eat bread made without yeast, as I commanded you. Do this at the appointed time in the month of Abib,* for in that month you came out of Egypt."
Exodus 23:15

Having been warned in a dream, he withdrew to the district of Galilee, and he went and lived in a town called Nazareth.
Matthew 2:22-23

From the Gospels of Matthew and Luke

Matthew and Luke both write of Joseph taking his family to Nazareth, with certain differences. Matthew has them going there, seemingly for the first time, after Jesus' birth in Bethlehem and the flight into Egypt (Matthew 2:22-23). In Luke there is no mention of Egypt,

---

* Mid-March to mid-April

and the trip to Nazareth is described as a return to their hometown: *"When Joseph and Mary had done everything required by the Law of the Lord* [in Jerusalem], *they returned to Galilee to their own town of Nazareth"* (Luke 2:39). The two Gospel writers have the family going to Nazareth at markedly different times. Indeed, the difference could be as much as several years depending on the time spent in Egypt. We must remember that details important to one writer were not necessarily important to other writers. They were not writing history but writing stories with a common theme of the deeper truth about Jesus, the Messiah.

In Matthew's account, it seems probable that the Holy Family upon returning from Egypt was heading for the district of Judea, either to Jerusalem or to Joseph's ancestral town of Bethlehem, which was nearby. It would have been attractive to be so near the Temple. However, Joseph soon learned of a new threat:

> *When he heard that Archelaus was reigning in Judea in place of his father Herod, he was afraid to go there. Having been warned in a dream, he withdrew to the district of Galilee, and went there and lived in a town called Nazareth.*
>
> Matthew 2:22-23

Rumors among the populace that the young child Jesus, "the King of the Jews," had returned might reach Archelaus. Mary and Joseph could not risk any danger to Jesus. Instead, Joseph moved his family to Nazareth, a small village north of Judea in the district of Galilee. Once again, we realize how critical Joseph's role was in salvation history! He trusted the angels who appeared in his dreams. He and Mary were united in their desire to do what God expected of them and to raise the son he had entrusted to them. Joseph could not risk his family's safety by living in Judea with Archelaus in power. The words Moses spoke to Joshua long before could also be said to apply to Joseph and his family: *"Do not be afraid or terrified because of them, for the Lord your God goes with you; he will never leave you nor forsake you"* (Deuteronomy 31:6).

Matthew and Luke provide no details about the Holy Family's life in Nazareth, but it can be assumed that for Mary, Joseph and Jesus, life there became as normal as possible in a land occupied by Roman forces. Nazareth was an out-of-the-way village. It may have received only cursory interest from Roman troops, except when needed to enforce the authority of the tax collector. Mary surely continued to devote herself to the care of her family and raising Jesus. She must have thought of the many incredible events that had occurred and wondered what lay ahead. But how could she know? As Megan McKenna writes, "Mary is a believer, not a knower."[28] As Jesus grew up, however, she must have observed how insightful and sensitive to others her son was becoming.

It may not have been an easy time or place to raise a child. The Roman forces levied burdensome taxes, and punishment for failure to pay was swift and harsh. However, Rome generally brought stability to the regions it governed.

Do we too easily imagine their hometown as an idyllic country village? Houses were humble abodes. Walls were most likely made of local stones. Roofs were fashioned from wood, mud and thatch. Water had to be hauled from a spring or well and cooking was done outside. Of course, there were no interior sanitation systems. Animals were sheltered inside the home when necessary. One significant blessing was that Joseph could use his carpentry skills to make their home as comfortable as possible.

Faith and the blessings of family may have eased their day-to-day struggles. The Jewish family structure was strong, with the mother at the center of every home. Mary's parents had raised her to be a faithful and loving woman obedient to Mosaic Law. Young Jesus was nurtured and taught by Mary and Joseph in the same way. Jesus was both human and divine, but his human nature had to be taught, and there is no better teacher than a loving mother.

As Jesus grew up, guided and nurtured by Mary, he must also have been trained in carpentry by Joseph, perhaps at first by fetching tools and materials for his father. It is not hard to imagine Jesus following his father around the village and neighboring towns as Joseph worked on various jobs. He would have observed the people whom they encountered: the young and the old, the kind and the unkind, those who were well and those who were sick.

Jesus would have witnessed much of the poverty, illness and disease found in the countryside—scenes he would not forget. In his novel *A Life of Jesus*, Shusaku Endo describes an aspect of village life that Jesus would have observed when working with his father:

> In summertime many people were bothered with eye trouble caused by a combination of flying dust and the intense ultra-violet sunlight. Victims of leprosy, too, appear in the Bible, and the lepers gathered together and shaved their heads, and were forced to live apart from any town or village.[29]

Reading Endo's description, one is reminded of the compassionate miracle Jesus later performed when a leper begged for his help: *"Lord, if you are willing, you can make me clean,"* to which Jesus responded, *"I am willing ... Be clean!"* (Matthew 8:2-3; see also Luke 5:12-13).

For the Holy Family, religion permeated daily life. The doorpost of their home was undoubtedly marked with a *mezuzah*, a roll of parchment inside a tube with the fundamental Jewish prayer, the Shema: "Hear, O Israel; the Lord our God, the Lord is one."[30] Joseph would have taken Jesus with him to the local synagogue. As historian Robert Aron writes, "In all likelihood he took him there at least three times a week: on the Sabbath (Friday evening and Saturday) and on the two other days—Monday and Thursday—when the Torah was read."[31] Jesus would have learned the Jewish faith from the Torah and other sacred texts, prayers and traditions.

Luke notes that Mary and Joseph traveled to Jerusalem every year for Passover (Luke 2:41) and relates an incident that occurred when Jesus was twelve years old and went with them on this trip. It is unclear if Jesus had previously accompanied them or if this was his first trip to Jerusalem since being presented in the Temple as an infant. I imagine that he would always have accompanied his parents, as Mary would not have wanted to be separated from him. As the boy grew, he undoubtedly learned much from these experiences with his parents.

It has been said that the most demanding job of all is being a parent. Those who have had this job can certainly empathize with Mary and Joseph! Being in Jerusalem to celebrate Passover and the Seder meal must have been a happy occasion for the Holy Family. When the festival was over and their religious obligation had been fulfilled, it was time to return to Nazareth. Groups would travel together for safety and fellowship. Women tended to walk together, and men did the same. Evidently, Mary and Joseph each thought Jesus was with the other group, but he was not. After a day's journey they could not find him among the travelers. Rushing back to Jerusalem, they searched for him there for three days. It is not hard to imagine their distress at being separated from their son in this way. The long-awaited Messiah, now a boy of twelve, was lost.

This was the first time we read of Mary being separated from Jesus. She and Joseph must both have been deeply troubled over the incident. I can imagine Joseph trying to remain calm for his wife's sake. He had to think clearly about where to search. In addition, they had to find a place to sleep. Did Joseph sleep at night or did he continue searching even at night? Would Mary allow herself to sleep or even to rest?

Finally, Mary and Joseph found him at the Temple, calmly interacting with the teachers there. Luke first notes how the others perceived Jesus: *"Everyone who heard him was amazed at his understanding and his answers"* (Luke 2:47). He then describes Mary and Joseph's reaction: *"When his parents saw him, they were astonished"* (Luke 2:48). We can hear the anguish in Mary's voice as she asked, *"Son, why have you treated us like this? Your father and I have been anxiously searching for you"* (Luke 2:48). But Jesus only answered, *"Why were you searching for me? ... Didn't you know I had to be in my Father's house?"* (Luke 2:49). It was a rather abrupt answer. Mary must have felt hurt by his rebuke and by his insensitivity to their feelings as they searched for him. How were they to know at this point in his life that he was responding to God's will for him? As Luke writes, *"They did not understand what he was saying to them"* (Luke 2:50).

Mary must have pondered her son's words. Clearly a change was occurring in Jesus. This was a seminal event! Perhaps she recalled the angel Gabriel's words: *"The holy one to be born will be called the Son of God"* (Luke 1:35). Perhaps she wondered if her son's mission was emerging even at this young age. Luke says, *"His mother treasured all these things in her heart"* (Luke 2:51). Despite her profound love for her son, being his mother was not always easy. As Elizabeth A. Johnson writes in her book *Dangerous Memories*, "The joy and the suffering together are facets of love, which is expressed in the paradoxical mix of relief and anger that parents experience after danger has passed."[32]

We wonder what the two parents said to Jesus on their way home, and he to them. All we know from Scripture is that *"he went down to Nazareth with them and was obedient to them ... And Jesus grew in wisdom and stature, and in favor with God and men"* (Luke 2:51-52). During the journey home of several days and nights, I imagine that they were each absorbed in their own thoughts. Mary must have recognized that her relationship with Jesus was changing. He was becoming less dependent upon her as he matured and began to perceive his mission. Joseph may have thought about his son's exchanges with the teachers in the Temple, who were amazed at the boy's insights. Perhaps he began to realize that in some ways their roles would reverse, with the father now learning from the son.

What was Jesus himself thinking as they journeyed home to Nazareth? We can imagine how absorbed he had been in conversing with the teachers. We might wonder how he could be so unaware of his absence from his parents. Perhaps he thought of his mother's relief and rebuke when they found him in the Temple. Did he come to realize how she must have felt not knowing where her son was and whether he was safe? He likely intended no disrespect to his parents but was captivated by the experience of interacting with the teachers in the Temple. At such illuminating moments we can imagine that no other concerns would have intruded into his thoughts. Young Jesus was attentive to the Father's will in a newly concentrated way. It must have been a compelling experience. Was Jesus unusually quiet, reliving the Temple experience as the family made their way home? Did he share some of his thoughts as they walked, or did he keep them to himself?

Jesus was with Mary from conception until his public ministry began. It is important to emphasize this. Jesus was with his mother for thirty years and his public ministry was for three years! After the Temple incident, we hear no more in Scripture about Joseph. The presumption is that Joseph died sometime between Jesus' twelfth and thirtieth years. The task of raising Jesus, given to Joseph by God, was completed. He had kept Mary and Jesus safe from harm. He had provided for them in all the ways that a husband and father could. In both faith and trust he had been open and responsive to each call from God. It seems reasonable to think of Joseph living at least until Jesus was close to adulthood. Whenever Joseph died, Jesus would have become responsible for the care of his mother.

When Jesus was thirty, he and Mary were invited to attend a wedding in Cana. Jesus' disciples came along to be with him and to enjoy the wedding feast. Next, John's Gospel will tell us about the remarkable events that took place at that wedding.

Thoughts to Ponder

- Mary and Joseph were terribly stressed when Jesus disappeared from them for three days, only to find that he was in the Temple listening to the teachers and asking them questions. If you have children, have you also experienced challenges as they begin to chart their own course in life? How have you responded?

- Joseph said "yes" to God four times, as recounted by Matthew: (1) accepting Mary as his wife, (2) leaving Bethlehem and fleeing to Egypt to safeguard his family, (3) returning to Israel after Herod died and (4) bypassing Judea and going instead to Nazareth in Galilee to keep his family safe. Joseph listened to and followed God's will for him. Isn't that our challenge also? How do you discern God's will in your life?

- Each year on March 19 the Church celebrates the Feast of St. Joseph, Spouse of the Blessed Virgin Mary. On May 1 the Church celebrates the Feast of St. Joseph the Worker. He is also revered as the patron saint of fathers and carpenters.[33] Joseph's faith in God allowed him to respond to the messages brought to him from God. In love and faith, he guided, protected and provided for Jesus and Mary. Could there be a more perfect example of husband and father? Has there been a Joseph figure in your life?

- Children enter a new relationship with their parents when they become adults themselves. This was true for Jesus and Mary as well. First she led and taught Jesus; then she followed and learned from him. What have you learned from your adult son or daughter?

Chapter Eight
The Wedding Feast at Cana

When all Egypt began to feel the famine, the people
cried to Pharaoh for food. Then Pharaoh told all the
Egyptians, "Go to Joseph and do what he tells you."

Genesis 41:55

His mother said to the servants, "Do whatever he tells you."

John 2:5

From the Gospel of John

John's Gospel recounts the story of a wedding that heralded the beginning of Jesus' public ministry. To begin, I will paint a word picture of the event as we try to understand Mary at this important time in her life.

Mary was now in her mid-forties and apparently a widow. Jesus, his disciples and Mary were invited to a wedding in the village of Cana, a few miles north of Nazareth.* Much as they are now, weddings were a time to put work aside and to celebrate with family and friends. But in Mary's time, such celebrations could last as long as a week. Food and wine were provided in abundance.

Imagine the festivities: People are getting reacquainted with friends from other villages. They are eating and drinking, chatting and dancing. A few may be drinking a little too much. We can imagine Jesus mingling with the guests and perhaps joining in the dancing from time to time. Mary is talking with the other women and watching the young people enjoying themselves. But Jesus is always in her sight, the habit of a loving mother, even though her son is now a man. A little more than thirty years have passed since the Annunciation. Jesus and Mary have been together the entire time.

What do we know of Mary at this stage in her life? I imagine that those who knew her realized she was somehow different from them. Perhaps her eyes reflected an inner peace, as though she knew something they did not. People were drawn to her because of her gentle strength and accepting manner. Certain people have a charisma that draws others to them. Many of us have experienced this as we find ourselves drawn to the quiet peace that emanates from someone we have come to trust. So it must have been with those who knew Mary. They seemed to sense that their confidences were safe with her. Children gathered around her naturally.

Here at this happy celebration, all was well. Mary's heart was stirring as she watched her son and his friends enjoying themselves. Mary knew her son was God's chosen one. She had watched as he became increasingly reflective, meditative and prayerful. She could see that his life was changing and moving inexorably toward his messianic mission.

As the wedding celebration continued, Mary became aware that the hosts were running out of wine. How did she know this? Maybe

---

* In Cana ("place of reeds" in Hebrew), three small churches have been built to commemorate the wedding. One of these, a Franciscan church, is often referred to as the "Wedding Church" since many couples renew their marriage vows there, as my wife, Peggy, and I did during two pilgrimages to the Holy Land.

she overheard the servants talking about it, or maybe the bride's mother sought Mary out and asked for her advice.

To run out of wine at a wedding would have been a failure of hospitality and therefore deeply embarrassing. Mary desired to help in the only way she knew, by asking her son to help: *"When the wine was gone, Jesus' mother said to him, 'They have no more wine'"* (John 2:3). This was the turning point! Notice that Mary did not tell her son what to do; she simply explained the problem to him. She was calling him forward. At first he balked, saying, *"Dear woman, why do you involve me? ... My time has not yet come"* (John 2:4). But turning to the servants, she said with confidence, *"Do whatever he tells you"* (John 2:5). Did she expect a miracle? It is difficult to say. There is no evidence that he had performed a miracle before this time. But she clearly expected that he would be able to help. Interestingly, Jesus changed his mind and did as his mother requested.

There were six water jars nearby that could each hold twenty to thirty gallons. Jesus told the servants to fill them with water, then draw some out and take it to the master of the banquet. The master of the banquet was surprised at the wine's fine quality and said to the bridegroom, *"Everyone brings out the choice wine first and then the cheaper wine after the guests have had too much to drink; but you have saved the best wine till now"* (John 2:10).

The servants must have been puzzled at first by the strange orders given to them by a guest, then amazed as they realized they had just witnessed a miracle. Many others must have been equally amazed as word spread about what Jesus had done. His disciples, observing what he had done and tasting the wine just as others were doing, must have discussed it among themselves in some wonderment: *"Jesus thus revealed his glory, and his disciples put their faith in him"* (John 2:11). Was Mary amazed? One wonders. Early on, Mary learned that nothing was impossible with God. Perhaps the best we can say is that she would have been less surprised than the guests.

Why did Jesus turn the water into wine? Why perform a miracle at a wedding feast? Perhaps it was to honor his mother who had asked for his help, or to spare the bridal party embarrassment. A wedding feast is a time of happiness for the bride and groom and their families. It is the start of their new life together, a time of hope for the future. But it is more than that. Jesus shows us an active, compassionate presence in the lives of these villagers. His action was an act of love. As John tells us, *"God is love"* (1 John 4:16). And here we have it, in this village wedding celebration.

The fact that the miracle involved wine is important. Yes, wine was an everyday drink, safer than plain water. But it was also a festive, celebratory drink that had deep symbolic importance to the Jewish people. Genesis recounts how it was used to celebrate an important victory by Abram: *"Then Melchizedek king of Salem brought out bread and wine. He was priest of God Most High, and he blessed Abram"* (Genesis 14:18-19). The Psalmist wrote of *"wine that gladdens the heart of man"* (Psalms 104:15). And the prophet Isaiah declared, *"On this mountain the Lord Almighty will prepare a feast of rich food for all peoples, a banquet of aged wine—the best of meats and the finest of wines"* (Isaiah 25:6).

More significantly, the miracle at Cana foreshadowed much that was to come. Mark's Gospel describes Jesus' words and actions at the Last Supper: *"Then he took the cup, gave thanks and offered it to them, and they all drank from it. 'This is my blood of the covenant, which is poured out for many ... I will not drink again of the fruit of the vine until that day when I drink it anew in the kingdom of God'"* (Mark 14:23-25).

At the Last Supper, Jesus gave us the gift of his body and blood through the celebration of the Eucharist, present to us today when the priest says the Eucharistic prayer during Mass. He first blesses the bread, then says,

> By the mystery of this water and wine
> may we come to share in the divinity of Christ,
> who humbled himself to share in our humanity ...
>
> Blessed are you, Lord God of all creation.
> Through your goodness we have this wine to offer,
> Fruit of the vine and work of human hands.
> It will become our spiritual drink.[34]

From the Last Supper to the early days of Christendom to the Church of today, the sacrament of Holy Eucharist, the transubstantiation of bread and wine into the body and blood of Jesus, is our spiritual communion with Jesus.

The story of the miracle at Cana is told only in John's Gospel. It is not included in the three earlier Gospels. It is an important story since it describes what is thought to be his first public miracle, after which his disciples began to believe more deeply in Jesus. It was Mary who recognized that the time had come for Jesus to begin his public ministry. Author Jon Sweeny emphasizes her role: "Not only did Mary give birth to Jesus, and not only was she the first person to have faith in him and his mission, but she also was the one who presented Jesus [at Cana] to the world."[35] This decisive event is also the moment when his first disciple, his mother Mary, instead of holding him back to care for her, "released" him by calling him to begin his public ministry. Indeed, who now would provide for her? Was she now alone? With Mary's encouragement, Jesus' public mission of redemptive salvation began.

The last words spoken by Mary as recorded in Scripture are the astounding words she addressed to the wine stewards: *"Do whatever he tells you"* (John 2:5). Her entire life had been devoted to Jesus. Now that her son's messianic journey had begun, Mary fades into the background in Sacred Scripture. It was time for her to let Jesus go, even though she may have perceived that there was danger ahead. Mary was with him again at different times over the next three years and was with him at Calvary. Simeon's prophecy, *"And a sword will pierce your own soul too,"* would soon become a reality.

Thoughts to Ponder

- Mary became an advocate for the bridal party and interceded with Jesus when the wine ran out. He resisted but changed his mind when she told the servants, *"Do whatever he tells you."* By initiating this miracle, Mary released her son to begin his ministry. She also showed that she can advocate and intercede for us with her son. Have you ever prayed to Mary for intercession? Why or why not?

- Sooner or later parents must let their children go out into the world. The children may be gone physically but will always remain in their parents' minds and hearts. How difficult it must have been for Mary to let Jesus go after being together for thirty years! How much of his future did she perceive? How much of your own children's future do you perceive?

- Rabbi Lord Jonathan Sacks once said, "Science takes things apart to see how they work. Religion puts things together to see what they mean."[36] He was speaking of the importance of unity among father, mother and children. God put Jesus, Mary and Joseph together as a family to help each other both physically and spiritually. How do your family members help each other in our secular society?

- The rich, abundant wine Jesus provided at the wedding in Cana foreshadowed the wine he blessed and shared with his disciples three years later at the Last Supper. In Jesus' ministry, every action and teaching had purpose, from Cana to the Last Supper to Calvary. Eucharist is our everlasting gift from Jesus. What does that mean to you personally?

Chapter Nine

Jesus' Mother and Brothers

The people walking in darkness have seen a great light;
on those living in the land of the shadow of death a light has dawned.

Isaiah 9:2

They all joined together constantly in prayer, along with the
women and Mary the mother of Jesus, and with his brothers.

Acts 1:14

From the Gospels of Matthew, Mark, Luke and John

The episodes in Mary's life that we have discussed so far are described only in one or two Gospels. She appears in the accounts of Jesus' ministry from time to time, but never as the focus of attention. In contrast, all four Gospel writers recount the teachings of Jesus as well as many of the healing miracles that he performed during his ministry. Their accounts of his ministry are complementary in ways that allow us to move seamlessly from one Gospel to another. For example, the three synoptic writers (Matthew, Mark and Luke) all describe Jesus healing a man with leprosy and healing Peter's mother-in-law. The events are not recorded in the same order from one Gospel to the next. However, the accounts support each other in other important ways. In this chapter we consider an episode from Jesus' ministry that involves Mary and that appears in three of the four Gospels.

Following the Wedding at Cana, Jesus began his public ministry in Capernaum in the district of Galilee. John tells us that Mary went with him to Capernaum along with his brothers and disciples: *"After this he went down to Capernaum with his mother and brothers and his disciples. There they stayed for a few days"* (John 2:12). Why Capernaum? Perhaps because Peter lived there with his mother-in-law and earned his living as a fisherman on the Sea of Galilee.* It would seem likely that Jesus and Mary stayed in Peter's home. Jesus healed Peter's mother-in-law from a high fever, after which she rose from her bed and served him and his disciples (Matthew 8:14-15, Mark 1:29-31 and Luke 4:38-39).

During this early period in Jesus' ministry people were drawn to him in ever-increasing numbers. Stories of cures he had performed were circulating. Some came hoping for a cure, others out of curiosity. Many came because Jesus was teaching about love and compassion. Mark describes the phenomenon:

> *Jesus withdrew with his disciples to the lake, and a large crowd from Galilee followed. When they heard all he was doing, many people came to him from Judea, Jerusalem, Idumea, and the regions across the Jordon and around Tyre and Sidon.*
>
> Mark 3:7-8

Slowly a new message of hope was arising in the land. Was Mary

---

* Also referred to as the Sea of Tiberias and Lake Gennesaret.

among those who gathered to hear him? We do not know, but shortly we will discuss one such incident in which she was present.

As awareness of Jesus' teachings began to spread along with stories of healings, religious leaders were also hearing about Jesus. As Mark writes, *"The Pharisees went out and began to plot with the Herodians* [influential Jews] *how they might kill Jesus"* (Mark 3:6). Clearly, the religious leaders were growing anxious about this radically new ministry: *"And the teachers of the law who came down from Jerusalem said, 'He is possessed by Beelzebub! By the prince of demons he is driving out demons'"* (Mark 3:22). How very contradictory; Satan driving out Satan!

In this context, the three synoptic Gospels relate an episode in which Jesus' "mother and brothers" appear (Matthew 12:46-50, Mark 3:31-35 and Luke 8:19-21). As Mark relates, Jesus' preaching was so compelling that people flocked to him:

> *Then Jesus entered a house, and again a crowd gathered,*
> *so that he and his disciples were not even able to eat.*
> *When his family heard about this, they went to take*
> *charge of him, for they said, "He is out of his mind."*
>
> Mark 3:20-21

His family wanted to take him home for his own safety. They were aware that he was attracting many followers and causing concern among the religious leaders. *"Then Jesus' mother and brothers arrived. Standing outside, they sent someone in to call him. A crowd was sitting around him, and they told him, 'Your mother and brothers are outside looking for you'"* (Mark 3:31-32). Jesus replied, *"Who are my mother and my brothers? … Here are my mother and my brothers! Whoever does God's will is my brother and sister and mother"* (Mark 3:33-35). Luke puts it this way: *"My mother and brothers are those who hear God's word and put it into practice"* (Luke 8:21).

Is this a rebuke to his mother? No! It is clear that Jesus loved Mary. Mary knew Jesus was the promised Messiah. She knew how God had guided and protected them over the years. It is therefore difficult to believe that Mary came thinking he was *"out of his mind."* Even so, Mary may have been concerned for Jesus' physical safety considering the notoriety and concern his ministry was generating.

Importantly, Jesus was instructing the crowd that his followers bear a greater spiritual responsibility to God the Father and to each other than to their birth families. As Fr. Brown and colleagues explain, the teaching "tells us who [now] constitute Jesus' family—a family that for want of a better term we may call his 'eschatological family,' i.e., the family called into being by Jesus' proclamation of the kingdom."[37] Far from rebuking Mary, Jesus used the arrival of Mary and his brothers to make a point. Jesus was exhorting the people to listen to and do God's will. Mary's life was a living example of someone doing God's will for over thirty years! His point was that there are two groups of people. On the one hand are those who live their day-to-day lives in an ordinary way; good people, perhaps, but not particularly attentive to God's will. On the other hand are those who conscientiously strive to do God's will. These people form the "eschatological" family Jesus was describing. What does it mean to do God's will? Scripture study is an obvious starting point. A more basic answer is simply: *"Do whatever he tells you."*

At some point, Jesus and presumably Mary returned to his hometown. Luke provides a most vivid account:

> *Jesus returned to Galilee in the power of the Spirit, and news about him spread through the whole countryside. He taught in their synagogues, and everyone praised him. He went to Nazareth, where he had been brought up, and on the Sabbath day he went into the synagogue, as was his custom. And he stood up to read. The scroll of the prophet Isaiah was handed to him.*
>
> Luke 4:14-17

Unrolling it, Jesus selected a passage containing a prophecy of messianic preaching and healing:

The Spirit of the Lord is on me,
because he has anointed me
to preach good news to the poor.
He has sent me to proclaim freedom for the prisoners
and recovery of sight for the blind,
to release the oppressed,
to proclaim the year of the Lord's favor.

Luke 4:18-19 and Isaiah 61:1-2

Handing the scroll back, Jesus sat down. Perhaps this was to give people time to think about what he had read. Then, with everyone's rapt attention, he said, *"Today this scripture is fulfilled in your hearing"* (Luke 4:21). At first, the reaction from the crowd was very positive. *"All spoke well of him and were amazed at the gracious words that came from his lips"* (Luke 4:22). Where, they wondered, had he gained such wisdom? *"'Isn't this Joseph's son?' they asked"* (Luke 4:22). They had undoubtedly heard of the miracles he had performed in and around Capernaum. How could someone who grew up just as they did be so different in what he said?

Knowing they were perplexed, Jesus continued, saying, *"Surely you will quote this proverb to me: 'Physician, heal yourself! Do here in your hometown what we have heard that you did in Capernaum.' I tell you the truth ... no prophet is accepted in his hometown"* (Luke 4:23-24). Then Jesus reminded them of the stories of Elijah helping a pagan widow instead of Israeli widows (1 Kings 17:7-24) and of Elisha healing a Syrian of leprosy instead of Israelites who also had leprosy (2 Kings 5:1-14). It must have been unsettling to the people to hear Jesus talk of the prophets healing Gentiles instead of their fellow Jews.

How very difficult it was for them to think beyond their insular world. They would have none of it. Shock grew into suspicion, disbelief and anger. Why the anger? It was an example of group unwillingness to comprehend what Jesus had proclaimed. Instead, his words now seemed disruptive and even scandalous and blasphemous to them. They drove him out of town and took him to a cliff with the intention of throwing him off. Yet, as Luke says, *"He walked right through the crowd and went on his way"* (Luke 4:30).

Several things are at work here for us to think about. First, Jesus was in control of the situation. The events that were recorded concerning Jesus were not mere happenstance. They were deliberate and principal to his teaching. Second, we see how difficult it is for people to grasp the idea that all people are important to God— Gentile or Jew, rich or poor. The family of God is comprised of those who listen to his word and put it into practice, not just those who by birth belong to a certain favored group.

Let's return to Mark and consider the question of Jesus' brothers and sisters. Mark relates what the people of his hometown said about him on this occasion:

> *"Where did this man get these things? ... What's this wisdom that has been given him, that he even does miracles! Isn't this the carpenter? Isn't this Mary's son and the brother of James, Joseph, Judas and Simon? Aren't his sisters here with us?" And they took offense at him.*
> Mark 6:2-3

We should consider what is meant by brothers and sisters in this passage. Who were they and is it important? Mark even names Jesus' brothers, but not his sisters. Over the millennia, three principal explanations have been offered and we will discuss them here.

One explanation is that Joseph, older than Mary, had children from a previous marriage. But considering the strong bonds of Jewish family life, it seems strange that these step-siblings, if any, were never mentioned in the description of the Holy Family's early years.

Another possibility is that they were children of Mary and Joseph born after Jesus. But if they had had other children, those siblings would have shared the responsibility for the care of Mary after the death of Joseph, and then full responsibility after the death of Jesus. The same would be true if they were Mary's step-children. Yet Jesus, when he was dying, asked one of his disciples to look after Mary, not any blood-sibling. This supports the Church's teaching that Mary remained a virgin throughout her life.[38]

A more likely explanation is that "brothers" and "sisters" refer to other close relations of Jesus. The Greek word *adelphos*,[39] meaning either blood brother or kinsman, is used in both the Old and New Testaments and with both meanings. *The Dictionary of Mary* states, "In Semitic usage, the terms 'brother' and 'sister' are applied not only to children of the same parents but also to nephews, nieces, cousins, half-brothers and half-sisters."[40]

Just as Jesus applied these terms broadly, from the earliest days of the Church to the present time, his followers commonly refer to their Christian friends as brothers and sisters.

Although this chapter has focused principally upon the episode in which Jesus' mother and "brothers" came to find him and take him home, I have felt it necessary to at least touch upon the issue of his brothers and sisters. The study of Scripture often leads to questions that are seemingly unanswerable. But such study often enriches the spirituality of thoughtful Christians.

Thoughts to Ponder

- Many who listened to Jesus were not open to his teaching, perhaps because they would have had to change their ways. It is the same today. We have the freedom to hear the word of God and to act on it, or to turn away. It is for some a difficult choice. I have a friend who admitted not wanting to get too close to God, because he was fearful of what God might want from him. Nobody said being a Christian was easy. How much are you willing to change in order to follow Jesus?

- There are many issues in the Bible that raise questions, but whose answers are not critical to our understanding of Christ's teachings. For example, who were the Magi and how many were there? The question of whether Jesus had siblings is another example, and there are many more. These subordinate issues are interesting, but they are simply background to the story of salvation revealed in Scripture. How well do you sift the "wheat" from the "chaff" in your Scripture study?

- What Jesus was teaching and revealing was countercultural in his time. All people are formed in the culture of their time. To hear a voice calling us to a new way of life requires openness and a thirst for truth, especially when traditional religious leaders hold sway. Many of the leaders in Jesus' time could not break free of their traditions. They may have endeavored to faithfully follow the letter of the law but not necessarily the spirit of the law. Therefore, they were not open to a prophetic new voice. How open do you allow yourself to be?

Chapter Ten

Mary at Calvary and Beyond

But he was pierced for our transgressions, he was crushed
for our iniquities; the punishment that brought us peace
was upon him, and by his wounds we are healed.

Isaiah 53:5

As Jesus was saying these things, a woman in the crowd called out,
"Blessed is the mother who gave you birth and nursed you."

Luke 11:27

From the Gospels of Matthew, Mark, Luke and John

Mary, the first disciple of Jesus, knew from the time of the Annunciation that her son would play a unique role in the salvation of her people. As he grew in maturity and wisdom, she must have reflected ever more deeply on what this meant. Once he was engaged in his public ministry, Holy Scripture makes little reference to Mary. Soon after the Wedding at Cana, John says Jesus *"went down to Capernaum with his mother and brothers and his disciples"* (John 2:12). As we saw in the last chapter, she visited him at least one other time while he was preaching. These episodes suggest that Mary may have been with him at other times during his three-year ministry, but Scripture is silent on this point. We are simply left to wonder about Mary's presence during most of this period. Regardless of how often she was with him, she surely was aware of his teachings and the miracles he was performing through informal networks of friends and visitors. But she is not mentioned again until John tells us she was with Jesus at Calvary.

Near the end of his ministry, on the Sunday before Passover, Jesus entered Jerusalem to the adulation of crowds of people waving palms and shouting for joy. Their joy in welcoming Jesus would turn to sorrow before the week was over.

Jesus was aware of what was going to happen to him and had tried to prepare his disciples for it. On Thursday, following the Last Supper (Passover), Jesus went to the Mount of Olives and prayed, *"Father, if you are willing, take this cup from me; yet not my will, but yours be done"* (Luke 22:42). The following day he was unjustly tortured, condemned and crucified, as detailed by all four evangelists.

John writes that Mary was present as her son was dying: *"Near the cross of Jesus stood his mother,"* among other followers (John 19:25). Author Lisa Brenninkmeyer imagines Mary's response to seeing her son endure this cruel death: "She didn't shrink back from human suffering. She didn't shield her eyes when her Son was stripped, beaten, and crucified. She pressed into the suffering and stayed by His side, providing strength with her presence."[41] The passion of the son was also a passion for the mother. Mary followed Jesus throughout his earthly life ... all the way to Calvary!

We know how profoundly Mary loved Jesus. For thirty years they had been together, mother and son. She must have understood that there would be suffering ahead. The practice of crucifixion as a public punishment by Roman forces was well known to the people, but could Mary have foreseen that this terrible fate would befall her son? Throughout his ministry, Jesus had brought hope to the people. His teaching and his presence were compelling and people flocked to him. He healed, taught and ministered to them in so many compassionate ways. His very presence was a manifestation of his goodness and love. Every action was to bring them into relationship to the Father through him.

Yet despite his evident goodness and holiness, Jesus was crucified. In terrible agony on the cross, he recognized his mother and the disciple John:

> *When Jesus saw his mother there, and the disciple whom he loved standing nearby, he said to his mother, "Dear woman, here is your son," and to the disciple, "Here is your mother." From that time on, this disciple took her into his home.*
>
> John 19:26-27

The pain Mary felt as she endured the long hours of Calvary must have been intense, perhaps recalling to her mind what Simeon had told her many years earlier: *"And a sword will pierce your own soul too"* (Luke 2:35). What Jesus felt on her behalf, in addition to the physical and mental torment of the crucifixion itself, must also have been intense. James Martin, S.J., in his book *Jesus: A Pilgrimage*, offers this penetrating thought:

> So imagine Jesus's sadness at seeing his mother suffer. If anything could have tempted him to walk away from the cross, it may have been this. I can imagine him asking the Father, "I will drink this cup, but must she drink it too?"[42]

Is it any wonder that our hearts also go out to Mary? She is emotionally torn in two. As a mother, she is distressed for her son and the unjust pain he must bear. Conversely, with graced knowledge of who her son is, and with awareness of his mission and destiny, Mary also has absolute belief and hope in Jesus.

Mary from Cana to Calvary, by Beverly Paddleford
Whispering Winds Catholic Camp, Julian, California

The bronze statue created by American sculptor Beverly Paddleford movingly conveys the power of this moment. It shows Mary seated near the cross after Jesus' body has been taken down. She holds the crown of thorns to her breast as she recalls the terrible agony of her son's crucifixion and death. Yet Mary, more than anyone, is aware that Jesus is the chosen one of God with a messianic mission. Despite her suffering at his unjust death, she is aware that this is not the end, but a new beginning. Her hand is open and reaches out, inviting us to understand that her beloved son and our savior has given his life for us. Mary always leads us to Jesus.

The four gospels describe the death and burial of Jesus with varying details, but they all tell us what is most important for us to know: He is risen!

> "Do not be afraid, for I know that you are looking for Jesus, who was crucified. He is not here; he is risen, just as he said. Come and see the place where he lay. Then go quickly and tell his disciples: He has risen from the dead and is going ahead of you into Galilee."
>
> Matthew 28:5-7

Following the death, resurrection and ascension of Jesus, the apostles gathered in a discrete location, an upper room in Jerusalem, to choose a disciple to replace Judas.

> Those present were Peter, John, James and Andrew; Philip and Thomas, Bartholomew and Matthew; James son of Alphaeus and Simon the Zealot, and Judas son of James. They all joined together constantly in prayer, along with the women and Mary the mother of Jesus, and with his brothers.
>
> Acts 1:13-14

This is the last time we hear explicitly of Mary's presence. However, Mary may have been present with the apostles at least one other time. At Pentecost, fifty days after Passover, many were gathered. "When the day of Pentecost came, they were all together in one place" (Acts 2:1). Who were gathered? Certainly, the eleven original disciples plus the new one, Matthias. Although Scripture does not say that Mary was present, it seems reasonable that she would be there since she was present with the disciples earlier when Matthias was chosen. We can infer that there were others as well: "Now there were staying in Jerusalem God-fearing Jews from every nation under heaven. When they heard this sound [a violent wind] a crowd came together in bewilderment" (Acts 2:5-6). Tongues of fire descended upon the disciples and they were filled with the Holy Spirit. The disciples, or followers, of Jesus were becoming apostles, meaning those sent forth in fulfillment of the Great Commission of Jesus: *"Therefore go and make disciples of all nations, baptizing them in the name of the Father and of the Son and of the Holy Spirit"* (Matthew 28:19). Jesus gave them the ultimate assurance for this mission: *"And surely I am with you always, to the very end of the age"* (Matthew 28:20).

Mary now had to continue to live her life, but where? From the Gospel of John, we know she was entrusted to the care of the beloved disciple, in his home. Would that be in Jerusalem or in Ephesus? In Ephesus there are the remains of a house long thought to be where Mary lived. It is a revered pilgrimage site. The Augustinian nun and mystic Anne Catherine Emmerich (1774-1824) wrote of a vision she had of Mary's house in Ephesus.[43] This has encouraged the belief that it was Mary's last home.

On August 15 the Church celebrates the Solemnity of the Assumption of the Blessed Virgin Mary. In this way the Church honors her passage into heaven. In 1950, Pope Pius XII formally declared, "We pronounce, declare and define it to be a divinely revealed dogma that the Immaculate Mother of God, the ever Virgin Mary, having completed the course of her earthly life, was assumed body and soul into heaven."[44]

Thoughts to Ponder

- Once, on a pilgrimage to the Holy Land, we walked on the same path that Jesus had been forced to walk, to the Church of St. Peter in Gallicantu, the site where Jesus was first held after being arrested by the palace guards. A few disciples had followed him at a safe distance. Sr. Grace Ann Loperena, C.S.J., asked us, "How closely do you follow Jesus: side-by-side, a step behind or back where you think it's safe?" How closely do you follow Jesus and how has your "faith walk" changed over time?

- As the mother of Jesus, Mary was also his first disciple. She modeled a deep faith in Jesus. Others in our lives may do this as well. Who best models faith for you and how has that affected you?

- Luke writes that a woman who heard him preach once called out, *"Blessed is the mother who gave you birth and nursed you"* (Luke 11:27). Jesus loved his mother and we are invited to do likewise. Mary can be our advocate and intercede for us with Jesus if we will only ask her. What have you asked of Mary, either in times of joy or in times of sorrow?

- This book is about Mary, but it is also about God's gift of Jesus brought to us through the faith, trust and courage of Mary. St. Maximilian Kolbe once said, "Never be afraid of loving the Blessed Virgin Mary too much. You can never love her more than Jesus did."[45] We honor and venerate Mary, but we worship only God: Father, Son and Spirit. What place does Mary have in your prayer life and why?

Afterword

The Joyous Mystery

Give thanks to the Lord, for he is good;
his love endures forever.
Psalms 106:1, 107:1, 118:1, 136:1

God is love.
1 John 4:16

The idea that a Messiah would come to save the Israeli people was a core Jewish belief. It had been foretold long before by the prophets of the Old Testament, including Jeremiah, who lived between 626 and 586 B.C.:

> *"The days are coming," declares the Lord,*
> *"when I will raise up to David a righteous Branch,*
> *a King who will reign wisely*
> *and do what is just and right in the land.*
> *In his days Judah will be saved*
> *and Israel will live in safety.*
> *This is the name by which he will be called:*
> *The Lord Our Righteousness."*
> Jeremiah 23:5-6

In Old Testament times, God had established a covenant with the Jewish people to be their God, and they would be his people. Later,

God chose Moses to lead the people out from four hundred years of slavery in Egypt to Palestine, the Promised Land.

In New Testament times, Jews anticipated that a Messiah like King David would come and free them from Roman rule. The question was not if but when and how the prophecy would be fulfilled. They waited, unaware that's God's salvific plan was beginning in a remote village in northern Palestine.

Our family friend, Fr. Bill Elliott, often reminded us that our God is a God of surprises. Indeed he is! He chose a young peasant girl from the village of Nazareth in the district of Galilee to bear his son, Jesus, the incarnate Christ.

This book has been about Mary as she lived among us, but in a truer sense it is about the Messiah she brought into the world. She and the Holy Spirit gave us not a warrior king, but a king of love! Quite a distinction. We need only read the Gospels to appreciate the merciful works and teachings of Jesus and understand his message of love in action. And we revere Mary and Joseph because their lives were devoted to raising, teaching and safeguarding Jesus. Mary was his first disciple from the moment of his birth. Her life is a model of a life lived in faith, trust and love.

God chose Mary to be a primary participant in his plan for our redemption. Mary was herself born in a state of graced holiness. Yet she, like us, possessed free will. Visited by the angel Gabriel, Mary accepted God's invitation. She said, *"I am the Lord's servant ... May it be to me as you have said"* (Luke 1:38). She thus became the Mother of God. Throughout her life Mary experienced the full range of human emotions. Her courage was repeatedly challenged but it never failed.

Mary fulfilled her role in what we can call a joyous mystery, presenting the incarnate Christ to the world. Born to Mary, Jesus is of her own flesh and blood! Why did God choose to manifest himself in this way? For an answer we return to St. Thomas Aquinas: "In order that Christ's body might be shown to be a real body, He was born of a woman. In order that His Godhead might be made clear, He was born of a virgin." God chose this path to make his coming into our world believable.

Mary did not do it alone. Joseph, her husband, provider and

protector, guided his little family through many challenges, some of them life threatening. Four times he received direction from God, and four times he acted promptly and decisively. Day after day, Joseph fulfilled his obligation to care for his family. We can reasonably assume that he died before Jesus' ministry began, because we hear no more of him in Scripture past the time when Jesus was in his teens. Joseph is indeed the paradigm for all husbands and fathers.

When did Mary leave this earthly life? We do not know, but she took all her human experiences with her to heaven. Because of who she is, what she experienced and where she is now, she is our advocate. When we come to know Mary more deeply by learning of her character and the challenges she met and the joys and sorrows that she experienced, we understand more profoundly her role as the mother of Jesus. The vector of her life always leads us to Jesus. It is little wonder, then, that there is such worldwide devotion to Mary.

As we have seen, details of Mary's life are sparse in the New Testament, particularly in the Gospel of Mark. Aside from the early years described in the Gospels of Matthew and Luke, and the Cana wedding story and Christ's passion in John's Gospel, Mary's presence is rarely mentioned. Perhaps that is the reason many Protestant churches have a more reserved reverence for Mary and her role in salvation history. For Roman Catholics, Anglicans and Eastern Orthodox Catholics, it is different. From the middle of the first century onward, the role of Mary in God's plan for our redemption has been pondered, prayed over, debated and more fully appreciated. For example, today we comfortably think of Mary as the Mother of God. Yet that designation came only after several hundred years of prayerful study and reflection. People of good faith in the Eastern and Western Churches worked diligently to understand and to express the deeper meaning of Mary's role in salvation history. Recall that the Church depends upon Holy Scripture, tradition and exegesis. All three are critical to understanding our faith. Scripture is the primary source for understanding Mary's life. Church traditions such as feast days, May devotions, the Rosary and shrines can enrich our appreciation of Mary. Careful study, or exegesis, has resulted in numerous enlightened works about Mary from throughout the Christian community.

Scripture is indeed the bedrock of our faith. However, as St. Augustine wrote, "There are truths on which Scripture is silent, but not reason. Of these is the Assumption of Blessed Mary."[46] Over the centuries various Church councils, such as the Council of Nicaea in 325 A.D., were convened to clarify and define Catholic beliefs in the Trinity. Similarly, the Council of Ephesus in 431 sought to clarify the understanding of Mary as Mother of God. In other words, Holy Scripture and tradition, along with time, reason, study and prayer have resulted in an ever-fuller understanding of Scripture and of Mary's importance.

But this book is not a theological treatise. As Jon Sweeney reminds us, "Mary doesn't want to be a theological argument. She's not a sticking point. She is the Mother of God and a mother for all of us."[47] Even so, it is important to understand Mary's unique role in salvation history, which is well articulated in this passage by Fr. Wilfrid Stinissen, O.C.D.:

> The New Covenant begins at the Annunciation. The dialogue between the angel and Mary presented by Saint Luke … is without doubt the most important dialogue that has ever taken place. The entire Old Covenant is a preparation for this conversation, and the New Covenant has been made possible only by Mary's Yes in this dialogue. Who could comprehend that God would lay such immense responsibility on one single person?[48]

Consider, then, these summary observations:

First, Mary is the keystone between the Old and New Testaments. A young Jewish peasant girl became the living bridge between the Old Testament prophecy of the coming Messiah and the New Testament fulfillment of that prophecy. Mary accepted God's invitation to bear a child by the Holy Spirit, a child of her own flesh and blood. In awe, we appreciate that she did so of her own free will, in faith, trust and love of God. It was through Mary's decision to say "yes" that the New Covenant through Christ Jesus could begin.

Second, Mary relied strongly on her faith in God, not knowing what was ahead for her. She had to face her parents, Joseph and the community as a pregnant woman with an explanation that was, at best, hard to believe. Later, with Joseph, Mary had the responsibility of raising Jesus, nurturing him and teaching him as he grew. They had the responsibility of protecting him from harm, even from those seeking to kill him. It was a daunting task for a poor couple living in a land occupied by Roman forces. But with God's grace, Mary and Joseph accomplished it.

Third, Mary and Joseph presented their son to God in the Temple as prescribed in the Torah. Blessed in the Temple rite, Jesus was then returned to his parents. Thus began his journey from infant to adulthood and the fulfillment of his mission. There on the Temple grounds, the child Jesus was recognized by Simeon and Anna for who he was: the long-awaited Messiah. Mary invites us to do the same.

Fourth, Mary called Jesus forward to begin his public ministry. At Cana, she established that she could be an advocate and intercede with her son. He said his time had not yet come, but Mary told the servants, *"Do whatever he tells you"* (John 2:5). Jesus changed his mind after hearing his mother, and thus the wedding celebration continued with the miracle of rich, abundant wine. His disciples began to believe in Jesus with a deeper awareness. Mary's injunction, *"Do whatever he tells you,"* extends to us as well.

Fifth, Mary was with her son from his birth to his death. Jesus, in agony on the cross, showed his deep love for his mother when he gave her to the care of his beloved disciple, John: *"When Jesus saw his mother there, and the disciple whom he loved standing nearby, he said to his mother, 'Dear woman, here is your son,' and to the disciple, 'Here is your mother'"* (John 19:26-27). To follow Jesus is also to honor Mary.

Sixth, we need to appreciate Mary not just as the Blessed Virgin, but in the fullness of her authentic human life: as daughter, cousin, wife, mother, refugee, widow, disciple and witness to her son's passion, death and resurrection. Graced by God, she nonetheless had to live with trust in the joyful mystery unfolding between heaven and earth.

The events in her life are compelling spiritual events that illuminate the ministry of her son. That is the beauty of Mary's life and example.

Reflect then upon the joyous mystery of God in our own lives. God manifested his love for humankind through Mary, the mother of our redeemer. Mary is at the heart of the story of our salvation. Without Mary there is no story as we are privileged to know it and to live it.

Appendix A

Annunciation and Nativity: Comparing Matthew and Luke

	Annunciation					Nativity			
	To whom	By whom	Context	Message	Instruction	Birthplace	Visitors	Animals	Journeys
Matthew	Joseph (1:20)	An angel (1:20)	In a dream (1:20), by implication in Joseph's home in Bethlehem (no mention of a home in Nazareth until they return from Egypt, 2:19-23)	Mary is with child through the Holy Spirit (1:20)	Joseph is to name him "Jesus" for he will save his people, and he will be called Emmanuel (God with us, 1:21-23)	Bethlehem (no mention of an inn or manger, 2:4-9)	Magi, guided by a star (2:1-12)	None mentioned	After the birth in Bethlehem the Holy Family flee to Egypt (2:13-15) and eventually to Nazareth (2:19-2; Joseph takes them to Nazareth out of fear of Archelaus)
Luke	Mary (1:26-32)	The angel Gabriel (1:26)	Gabriel appears to Mary in Nazareth (1:26)	The Holy Spirit and the power of the Most High over-shadow Mary (1:35)	Mary is to name him "Jesus." He will be called Son of the Most High (1:31-32)	In a manger in Bethlehem, for there was no room in the inn (2:7)	Shepherds, after being informed by angels where to find him (2:15-20)	None mentioned	From Nazareth to Bethlehem before the birth, then a return to Nazareth (2:1-4, 22, 39)

Adapted from *Hail Mary, Holy Bible* by Clifford M. Yeary. ©2017 by Order of Saint Benedict. Published by Liturgical Press, Collegeville, Minn. Used with permission.

Appendix B

The Canticle of Zechariah

From the Gospel of Luke

Following the circumcision and naming of John, his father, Zechariah, offered a song of praise and prophecy, which is one of three "canticles" in the Gospel of Luke. Others are Mary's Magnificat and Simeon's Nunc Dimittis discussed in Chapters 3 and 5, respectively.

This prayer is the culmination of all the remarkable experiences Zechariah had had over the previous nine months. While serving in the Holy of Holies, he was visited by an angel who told him his elderly wife, Elizabeth, would bear him a son, John, who would be *"great in the sight of the Lord"* (Luke 1:15). Zechariah challenged the angel, saying, *"How can I be sure of this? I am an old man and my wife is well along in years"* (Luke 1:18). For his disbelief, he was struck dumb. Even so, Elizabeth did become pregnant, and six months into her pregnancy the couple received Elizabeth's cousin Mary into their household. Finally, his son was born. As soon as Zechariah confirmed, by writing, that the boy would be named John, his power of speech returned. Moved by the birth of his son, and by his awareness of Mary's condition, he offered a deeply felt prophetic prayer:

> *"Blessed be the Lord, the God of Israel;*
> > *for he has visited and brought redemption to his*
> > > *people.*
> *He has raised up a horn for our salvation*
> > *within the house of David his servant,*

even as he promised through the mouth of his holy
prophets from of old:
salvation from our enemies
and from the hand of all who hate us,
to show mercy to our fathers
and to be mindful of his holy covenant
and of the oath he swore to Abraham our father,
and to grant us that, rescued from the hand of
enemies,
without fear we might worship him
in holiness and righteousness before him all our days.

"And you, child, will be called prophet of the Most
High,
for you will go before the Lord to prepare his ways,
to give his people knowledge of salvation
through the forgiveness of their sins,
because of the tender mercy of our God
by which the daybreak from on high will visit us
to shine on those who sit in darkness
and death's shadow,
to guide our feet into the path of peace."

Luke 1:68-79 (NAB Revised)[49]

The Canticle of Zechariah remains important to us today because it provides a sense of hope. Zechariah first praises God in gratitude and then moves to the promise of salvation through the House of David. He reaches back to earlier times and the promises of the prophets and to Abraham. Then he presciently refers to his son John preparing the way for the Lord. Zechariah expresses great hope for his people and his son. Today, his canticle is prayed each morning as a part of the Church's morning prayers, a testament to Zechariah's place in salvation history.

Suggested Reading

There are several very accessible works about Mary that readers of this book may enjoy:

Calloway, Donald. *Mary of Nazareth: The Life of Our Lady in Pictures.* San Francisco: Ignatius, 2014.

Exquisite pictures from the film *Mary of Nazareth,* directed by Giacomo Campiotti.

Hahn, Scott. *Hail, Holy Queen: The Mother of God in the Word of God.* New York: Image, 2001.

Written by a popular Catholic theologian and teacher, formerly a Presbyterian minister. Describes his wonder at discovering Mary's place in salvation history.

Johnson, Elizabeth A. *Dangerous Memories: A Mosaic of Mary in Scripture.* New York and London: Continuum, 2006.

Written by a scholar theologian with a clear and graceful writing style. Brings the Gospel stories alive in refreshing ways. Never invents, but searches for deeper meanings.

Miravalle, Mark. *Meet Mary: Getting to Know the Mother of God.* Manchester, N.H.: Sophia, 2007.

Written by a noted Mariologist who provides, for Christian and non-Christian readers alike, an explanation of the Catholic devotion to Mary.

Sheen, Fulton J. *The World's First Love: Mary, Mother of God.* San Francisco: Ignatius, 1952.

A classic work on the meaning of Mary's life, then and now.

Stinissen, Wilfrid. *Mary in the Bible and in Our Lives*. Translated by Sr. Clare Marie. San Francisco: Ignatius, 2006.

Written by a Carmelite monk following years of contemplative prayer and study. A review of Catholic Marian beliefs rooted in Sacred Scripture and Church exegesis.

Sweeney, Jon M. *Strange Heaven: The Virgin Mary as Woman, Mother, Disciple, and Advocate*. Brewster, Mass.: Paraclete, 2006.

A comprehensive survey of Mary's life and of Mariology from ancient times to the present. Covers a range of topics, including Martin Luther's love of Mary, Marian myths and legends, dogmas of the Church and more.

Yeary, Clifford M. *Hail Mary, Holy Bible: Sacred Scripture and the Mysteries of the Rosary*. Collegeville, Minn.: Liturgical, 2016.

Rosary meditations based on in-depth Biblical study.

Three other scholarly works are invaluable resources on the role of Mary in Holy Scripture:

Brown, Raymond E. *The Birth of the Messiah*. Garden City, N.Y.: Doubleday, 1977.

The definitive work on the nativity stories by the foremost American Scripture scholar in recent times. Explores both the Matthean and Lucan infancy narratives. Intended for theologians and researchers.

Brown, Raymond E., Karl P. Donfried, Joseph A. Fitzmyer and John Reumann, editors. *Mary in the New Testament: A Collaborative Assessment of Mary by Protestant and Catholic Scholars*. Philadelphia: Fortress, 1978.

Sponsored by the United States Lutheran-Roman Catholic Dialogue. Discusses both shared and divergent points of view.

Graef, Hilda. *Mary: A History of Doctrine and Devotion*. Notre Dame, Ind.: Christian Classics, 2009.

A comprehensive survey of Mariology.

Acknowledgments

As author I take responsibility for the claims and opinions expressed in this book. I did, however, burden several special people with reviewing successive drafts. Foremost among these was my late wife, Peggy. She read, edited and commented on all the early drafts, and there were many!

Our daughter, Sr. Karen Marie Anderson, F.S.P., reviewed an early draft while on home leave from Rome. With her editorial background, her comments were very helpful. Sr. Joan Henehan, C.S.J., reviewed the next draft, making many useful comments.

Deacon Peter Hodsdon, a scholar, skilled homilist, author and friend, was the next to review the manuscript. His comments were clear, insightful and valuable. He also recommended additional source materials that were very useful. As an extra gift, Peter asked his wife, Katie Hodsdon, to do a read-through. I happily add my thanks for her insightful comments.

In late 2018, Sr. Karen was again on home leave from Rome. She graciously took up a red pen again and read through the penultimate draft, making critical suggestions.

Researching, writing and revisions continued until finally it was in the hands of our son, Christopher Anderson, a skilled and challenging editor. Each week as we worked together on the book, we had wonderful and far-reaching discussions. The time spent in those discussions was for me a gift beyond price.

GBA

References

1   Sweeney, Jon M. *Strange Heaven: The Virgin Mary as Woman, Mother, Disciple, and Advocate.* Brewster, Mass.: Paraclete, 2006, pg. 147.

2   Augustine. Quoted in Scott Hahn, *Hail, Holy Queen: The Mother of God in the Word of God.* New York: Image, 2001, pg. 21.

3   Brown, Raymond E. *The Birth of the Messiah: A Commentary on the Infancy Narratives in Matthew and Luke.* Garden City, N.Y.: Doubleday, 1977, pg. 497.

4   Campiotti, Giacomo, director. *Mary of Nazareth.* San Francisco: Ignatius, 2013. DVD.

5   Barker, Kenneth L., et al., editors. *NIV Study Bible, Fully Revised.* Grand Rapids, Mich.: Zondervan, 2002.

6   Brown. *The Birth of the Messiah*, pg. 268.

7   Barclay, William. *The Gospel of Luke, Revised Edition.* Philadelphia: Westminster, 1975, pg. 17.

8   Martin, James. *Jesus: A Pilgrimage.* New York: HarperOne, 2014, pg. 75.

9   Isbouts, Jean-Pierre. *In the Footsteps of Jesus: A Chronicle of His Life and the Origins of Christianity.* Washington: National Geographic, 2012, pg. 90.

10 Mathews, Marcia M. *Henry Ossawa Tanner: American Artist.* Chicago and London: Univ. of Chicago, 1969, pg. 94.

11 Bruce, Marcus C. *Henry Ossawa Tanner: A Spiritual Biography.* New York: Crossroad, 2002, pg. 132.

12 Bernard of Clairvaux. Adapted from "In Praise of the Virgin Mother," Hom. 4:8-9; *Opera omnia*, Edit. Cisterc 4, 1966, pgs. 53-54. Quoted in *Office of Readings for Advent*, December 20. http://www.liturgies.net/Liturgies/Catholic/loh/advent/december20or.htm. Accessed June 29, 2019.

13 Sweeney. *Strange Heaven*, pg. 39.

14 Campiotti. *Mary of Nazareth.*

15 Rolheiser, Ronald. *An Anatomy and Theology of Trust ... Moving from Paranoia to Metanoia.* Los Angeles: Los Angeles Religious Education Congress, 2011. CD 1-19.

16 Aquinas, Thomas. Quoted in Scott Hahn, *Hail, Holy Queen: The Mother of God in the Word of God.* New York: Image, 2001, pg. 102.

17 Hock, Ronald F. *The Infancy Gospels of James and Thomas.* Santa Rosa, Calif.: Polebridge, 1995, pg. 49.

18 Sheen, Fulton J. *The World's First Love*. San Francisco: Ignatius, 1996, pgs. 95-6.

19 Sheen. *The World's First Love*, pg. 96.

20 Sweeney. *Strange Heaven*, pgs. 25-6.

21 Aquinas. In Hahn, *Hail, Holy Queen*, pg. 102.

22 Miravalle, Mark. *Meet Mary: Getting to Know the Mother of God*. Manchester, N.H.: Sophia, 2007, pg. 43.

23 Hock. *The Infancy Gospels of James and Thomas*, pg. 77.

24 Brown. *The Birth of the Messiah*, pgs. 170-3.

25 Barclay, William. *The Gospel of Matthew, Vol. 1*. Philadelphia: Westminster, 1975, pg. 33.

26 McKenna, Megan. *Mary: Shadow of Grace*. Hyde Park, N.Y.: New City, 2007, pg. 70.

27 Josephus. *The Works of Josephus*. Translated by William Whiston. Peabody, Mass.: Hendrickson, 1991, pg. 461.

28 McKenna. *Mary: Shadow of Grace*, pg. 63.

29 Endo, Shusaku. *A Life of Jesus*. Translated by Richard A. Schuchert. New York: Paulist, 1978, pg. 11.

30 Aron, Robert. *A Boy Named Jesus*. Berkeley, Calif.: Ulysses, 1997, pg. 34.

31 Aron. *A Boy Named Jesus*, pg. 42.

32 Johnson, Elizabeth A. *Dangerous Memories: A Mosaic of Mary in Scripture*. New York and London: Continuum, 2006, pg. 136.

33 Butler, Alban. *Lives of the Saints*. New York: Gallery, 1990, pg. 50.

34 International Commission on English in the Liturgy. *The Roman Missal, Third Edition*. Collegeville, Minn.: Liturgical, 2011, pgs. 529-30.

35 Sweeney. *Strange Heaven*, pg. 49.

36 Sacks, Jonathan. "The Love That Brings New Life Into the World." *Columbia Magazine*. May 2015. Vol. 95, no. 5, pgs. 12-15.

37 Brown, Raymond E., et al., editors. *Mary in the New Testament: A Collaborative Assessment by Protestant and Roman Catholic Scholars*. Philadelphia: Fortress, 1978, pg. 53.

38 United States Conference of Bishops. *United States Catholic Catechism for Adults*. Washington: US Conference of Bishops, 2006, pg. 144.

39 Brown. *Mary in the New Testament*, pg. 65.

40 *Dictionary of Mary, Revised Expanded Edition*. Totowa, N.J.: Catholic Book, 2013, pg. 313.

41 Brenninkmeyer, Lisa. "Comforting Mercy." In *Beautiful Mercy: Experiencing God's Unconditional Love So We Can Share It With Others*. Erlanger, Ky.: Dynamic Catholic, 2015, pgs. 95-6.

42 Martin. *Jesus: A Pilgrimage*, pg. 390.

43 Emmerich, Anne Catherine. *The Life of the Blessed Virgin Mary*. Translated by Michael Palairet. Charlotte, N.C.: TAN, 2013, pgs. 357-89.

44 Pius XII. Quoted in Sweeney, *Strange Heaven*, pg. 154.

45 Kolbe, Maximilian. "Saint Maximilian Kolbe Quotes." *The Catholic Reader*, June 11, 2013. http://thecatholicreader.blogspot.com/2013/06/st-maximilian-kolbe-quotes.html. Accessed June 29, 2019.

46 Augustine. Quoted in Hilda Graef, *Mary: A History of Doctrine and Devotion*. Notre Dame, Ind.: Christian Classics, 2009, pg. 175.

47 Sweeney. *Strange Heaven*, pg. 203.

48 Stinissen, Wilfrid. *Mary in the Bible and in Our Lives*. Translated by Sr. Clare Marie. San Francisco: Ignatius, 2018, pg. 21.

49 *The New American Bible with the Revised New Testament*. Iowa Falls, Iowa: World Bible, 1986.

CPSIA information can be obtained
at www.ICGtesting.com
Printed in the USA
LVHW011431260819
628943LV00021B/1346/P